Rosary Meditations
for Real Life
Volume I

Published by Real Life Rosary
PO BOX 390
Logan, OH 43138
www.realliferosary.com
www.jamesmhahn.blogspot.com

All scriptural texts are taken from the Douay-Rheims
translation unless otherwise noted. Every attempt has
been made to give credit where it is due.

To: My mother for giving me life.
My wife for showing me how to love.
Mary for leading me to her Son.

Acknowledgments

I would like to thank my wife Nicole for the support and encouragement in writing this book.

I would also like to thank Mr. and Mrs. David LeBlanc for their editing and critiquing of this work and for their prayers, love, and wonderful daughter.

I would like to thank my parents and brothers for their patience in this work and prayers for its success. I would also like to thank them for praying these mysteries with me. Those times of prayer in the sunroom were moments of grace for everyone.

Contents

How to Pray the Rosary

Begin by making the sign of the Cross with the Crucifix.

While holding the Crucifix pray the **Apostles Creed**

> *I believe in God, the Father Almighty, Creator of Heaven and Earth. And in Jesus Christ His only Son Our Lord who was conceived by the Holy Spirit, born of the Virgin Mary, suffered under Pontius Pilate, was crucified, died, and was buried. He descended into hell. On the third day He rose again and sits at the right hand of God, the Father Almighty, from thence He shall come to judge the living and the dead. I believe in the Holy Spirit, the Holy Catholic Church, the communion of saints, the forgiveness of sins, the resurrection of the body and life everlasting. Amen*

On the larger bead pray one **Our Father**

> *Our Father, who art in heaven, hallowed be Thy name. Thy kingdom come, Thy will be done on earth as it is in heaven. Give us this day our daily bread and forgive us our trespasses as we forgive those who trespass against us and lead us not into temptation but deliver us from evil. Amen.*

On the three smaller beads pray **Hail Marys** for an increase of Faith, Hope, and Charity

> *Hail Mary, full of grace. The Lord is with thee. Blessed art thou among women and blessed is the fruit of thy womb, Jesus. Holy Mary, mother of God, pray for us sinners now and at the hour of our death. Amen.*

Conclude the three beads with the **Glory Be**

> *Glory be to the Father and to the Son and to the Holy Spirit as it was in the beginning, is*

now, and ever shall be world without end.
Amen

On the next large bead announce the mystery and read the meditation.

After a moment of silent meditation begin the *Our Father.*
Continue by praying a *Hail Mary* on each of the smaller beads while meditating on the mystery and meditation.
  The additional clause may be inserted after the words "thy womb Jesus" to further enrich each meditation.
  Conclude each decade with a *Glory Be* and the
Fatima Prayer
  Oh my Jesus, forgive us our sins and save us
  from the fires of hell. Lead all souls into
  heaven. Help especially those who are in most
  need of thy mercy.
After all five decades are repeated pray the *Hail Holy Queen.*
  Hail Holy Queen, mother of Mercy, our life,
  our sweetness, and our hope. To thee do we
  cry poor banished children of Eve. To thee do
  we send up our sighs mourning and weeping in
  this valley of tears. Turn, then, most gracious
  advocate, thine eyes of mercy towards us and
  after this our exile show unto us the blessed
  fruit of thy womb, Jesus. O clement, O loving,
  O sweet Virgin Mary. Pray for us O holy
  mother of God, that we may be made worthy of
  the promises of Christ.

  Conclude with the following prayers and the sign of the Cross.

O God, Whose only begotten Son, by His life, death, and resurrection has purchased for us the rewards of eternal life, grant we beseech Thee, that meditating upon these mysteries of the most Holy Rosary of the Blessed Virgin Mary, we may imitate what they contain, and obtain what they promise: through the same Christ Our Lord. Amen.

V. May the Divine Assistance remain always with us.
R. And may the souls of the faithful departed rest in peace. Amen

St. Michael the Archangel, defend us in battle, be our defense against the wickedness and snares of the devil. May God rebuke him we humbly pray and do thou O Prince of the heavenly host, by the power of God, cast into hell Satan and all evil spirits who prowl about the world seeking the ruin of souls. Amen.

"The Rosary is said not with the lips alone, muttering Hail Marys one after the other. That is the way over pious old men and women rattle them off. For a Christian, vocal prayer must spring from the heart, so that while the Rosary is said, the mind can enter into contemplation of each one of the mysteries."

- St. Josemaria Escriva   *Furrow # 477*

Preface

This book is a product of my own desire to contemplate the mysteries of the Rosary more fully and an attempt to answer the call of Pope John Paul II to "…sit at the school of Mary and contemplate the beauty of the face of Christ and to experience the depths of His love"[1]. Here I have attempted to prove true that "…the simple prayer of the Rosary marks the rhythm of life."[2] Every aspect of our daily lives can be found in the "rhythm" of the Rosary. Our works, joys, sorrows, and desires are found in the mysteries of the Rosary. With careful contemplation of these mysteries we will find ourselves within the life of Mary, Jesus, and the Holy Trinity.

"Jesus Christ the Redeemer of man reveals man to man himself and brings to light his exalted vocation."[3] In the mysteries of the Rosary we can see ourselves. We can see Christ revealing to us who we are and who He wants us to be.

It is my prayer that this book will lead you to find the mysteries of the Rosary in your daily life. I also pray, with Mary, that you will find a new and more fruitful way in which to "contemplate the face of Christ".

May Jesus Christ be praised now and forever and may Mary, the Mother of Christ and the Mother of the Church, lead us to her Son now and at the hour of our death.

James M. Hahn

---

[1] Rosarium Virginis Mariae #1
[2] Angelus Message of Oct. 29, 1978
[3] Gaudium et Spes 22

The Mysteries of Work

"Work is man's original vocation. It is a blessing from God, and those who consider it a punishment are sadly mistaken.
The Lord, who is the best of fathers, placed the first man in Paradise *ut operaretur*, so that he would work."

- St. Josemaria Escriva   *Furrow # 482*

The Joyful Mysteries of Work

The Annunciation

...the angel Gabriel was sent from God to a city of Galilee named Nazareth, to a virgin betrothed to a man whose name was Joseph, of the house of David; and the virgin's name was Mary.

For what doth it profit a man, if he gain the whole world, and suffer the loss of his own soul? Or what exchange shall a man give for his soul? For the Son of man shall come in the glory of his Father with his angels: and then will he render to every man according to his works.

- Luke 1:26-27, Matthew 16:26-27

Mary was not sitting idle when the angel appeared. Traditional artwork shows Mary reading scripture, meditating on the word of God. The fact is Mary was serving God by working through the scriptures. Whether I work in an office, on a construction site or at home my work can bring me closer to God. Mary wasn't sitting idle waiting for a sign from God that she was to be the Mother of the Messiah. She was fulfilling her daily duties when God's message came. What will my state of mind be and what will I be doing when God's messenger comes? What if it is not a messenger but God Himself? Will I be humbly attending to the work set before me or will I be complaining against the task? "Be it done unto me."[1]

Our Father, Hail Mary, Glory Be, Etc.
Additional clause: ...of thy womb, Jesus,
who was conceived in you by the Holy Spirit

The Visitation

In those days Mary arose and went with haste into the hill country to a city of Judah, and she entered the house of Zechariah and greeted Elizabeth.

Neither do men light a candle and put it under a bushel, but upon a candlestick, that it may shine to all that are in the house. So let your light shine before men, that they may see your good works, and glorify your Father who is in heaven.

- Luke 1:39-40, Matthew 5:15-16

"Faith without works is dead"[2], says St. James. Mary's joy in being chosen as the Mother of God manifests itself in works of charity. She did not visit Elizabeth to flaunt her position or seek praise. She came to serve and to work. Imagine the Mother of the Creator doing menial household tasks. If Christ is truly in me, I will fulfill all my duties with joy. Even the most meaningless task at my daily job has meaning when I, like Mary, have Christ within me.

Lord, help me to imitate Mary as she imitates you in seeking to serve and not to be served.

Our Father, Hail Mary, Glory Be, etc.
Additional clause: ...of thy womb, Jesus,
whom you carried to Elizabeth

The Nativity

And in that region there were shepherds out in the field, keeping watch over their flock by night. And an angel of the Lord appeared to them, and the glory of the Lord shone around them, and they were filled with fear. And the angel said to them "Be not afraid.."

I know thy works, and thy faith, and thy charity, and thy ministry, and thy patience, and thy last works which are more than the former.

- Luke 2:8-10, Revelation 2:19

Here again are men doing what they are called to do when God reveals Himself. The shepherds were tending their flocks when the angels appeared, bringing the good news. They were in the midst of their work when God chose to speak to them. I too can hear God speaking to me as I go about my work. God has always intended man to work, even before the fall, "God took man, and put him in the paradise of pleasure, to dress it and to keep it."[3] My work can be my prayer, my communication with God. Paul tells me to, "Pray without ceasing."[4] This is possible when I offer my every working moment to God as a prayer.

Our Father, Hail Mary, Glory Be, Etc.
Additional clause: …of thy womb, Jesus,
who was born in Bethlehem

The Presentation

"Lord now lettest thy servant depart in peace, according to thy word; for mine eyes have seen thy salvation, which thou hast prepared in the presence of all peoples..."

Wherefore, my dearly beloved, (as you have always obeyed, not as in my presence only, but much more now in my absence,) with fear and trembling work out your salvation. For it is God who worketh in you, both to will and to accomplish, according to his good will. And do ye all things without murmurings and hesitations

- Luke - 2:29-31, Philippians 2:12-14

Simeon was faithful to his calling, faithful to his vocation. He did not call off work on the day of the Presentation. He did not call his boss and give him some lame excuse. Sure, God had promised him that he would see the Messiah, but Simeon couldn't just sit around and wait. He had to do something. Simeon was faithful to his work and God rewarded him, but God rewarded him toward the end of his life.

Often I imagine God's revelation, that he would see the Messiah, coming to Simeon when he is an old man. However, I must consider that this revelation could have come to Simeon when he was a very young man.

Am I faithful to my vocation even when I don't feel like it? How long will I wait to hear from God? A week? A year? My entire life? I can be faithful to God by fulfilling my duties patiently and by waiting on God until the appointed time.

Our Father, Hail Mary, Glory Be, Etc.
Additional clause: ...of thy womb, Jesus,
whom you presented in the Temple.

7

The Finding in the Temple

After three days they found him in the temple, sitting among the teachers, listening to them and asking them questions…and he went down with them and was obedient to them…

All things have their season, and in their times all things pass under heaven. A time to rend, and a time to sew. A time to keep silence, and a time to speak.

- Luke 2:46, 51, Ecclesiastes 3:1, 7

I would be remiss if I did not mention the man the Church calls, "the worker." Joseph says not one word in scripture. He neither exclaims nor complains. *In silentio et in spe erit fortitudo vestra* (in silence and trust shall be your strength).

Joseph endures all things quietly and patiently. When Joseph and Mary find the boy Jesus in the Temple after three days, "the worker" says nothing. However, if I read further, I find that Jesus was obedient to this man.

Do I complain about my job or vocation? Do I endure all things patiently as St. Paul says those who have love do?[5] Can I take time to imitate a man who endured all things in silence and trust, and loved so much as to have the Child Jesus be obedient to him? In silence and in trust was "the worker's" strength; it can be mine as well.

Our Father, Hail Mary, Glory Be, Etc.
Additional clause: …of thy womb, Jesus,
whom you found in the Temple.

The Luminous Mysteries of Work

The Baptism of Our Lord

"...who are you?" He confessed, he did not deny, but confessed, "I am not the Christ."...I am a voice of one crying in the wilderness, "Make straight the way of Lord," as the prophet Isaiah said.

Humble thy heart, and endure: incline thy ear, and receive the words of understanding: and make not haste in the time of clouds. Wait on God with patience: join thyself to God, and endure, that thy life may be increased in the latter end.

- John 1: 19-20, 23, Sirach 2:2-3

"Prepare ye the way of the Lord, make straight his paths."[6] What a task poor John had. He had been one of the first to recognize Christ even while still in the womb. I must recognize that that first encounter with Christ prepared the way for John. Many times my work seems overwhelming. Like John, I seem to get pressure from all sides. He not only had to "prepare the way" he also had to deal with the scholars and lawyers who were questioning him.

My work too can weigh heavily on me. During my day I must meet deadlines, deal with traffic, broken equipment, or crying babies, while attempting to remain strong in a world that tries to drain every ounce of energy from me. All of this can amount to very little if I have the right frame of mind. I must remember that I, like John, must decrease so that He might increase. My job everyday is to prepare the way of the Lord in the hearts of my family, friends, and co-workers. If I walk a straight path, those who see me may find the path is straight for them if they will only follow Christ.

Our Father, Hail Mary, Glory Be, Etc.
Additional clause: ...of thy womb, Jesus,
who was baptized by John.

9

The Wedding at Cana

His mother said to the servants, "Do whatever he tells you." Jesus said to them, "fill the jars with water." And they filled them to the brim. He said to them, "now draw some out and take it to the steward of the feast."

They were thirsty, and they called upon thee, and water was given them out of the high rock, and a refreshment of their thirst out of the hard stone.

- John 2:5, 7-8, Wisdom 11:4

How often I forget that God is in charge. How often I forget that God is God, and I am not, and all things from the air I breathe to the roof over my head is a gift from Him. This does not mean that I can do nothing, because Jesus wants to use me if I will allow Him. It is always my choice.

At the wedding at Cana Mary gives an instruction that should rule my daily life, especially at work. "Do whatever He tells you."[7] This message was addressed to the servants at the wedding but also to me, a servant of Christ. Those servants had no power of their own but through their obedience in their job many others were blessed by God.

If I am diligent and obedient in my work God can work miracles through me. If I do whatever He tells me, the water of this world can be turned into the wine of the kingdom. In other words, the common mundane tasks of my daily work can be transformed into a glorious example of God's love and concern for His children and those who thirst for holiness.

Our Father, Hail Mary, Glory Be, Etc.
Additional clause: …of thy womb, Jesus,
who transformed water into wine.

The Proclamation of the Kingdom

And Jesus, full of the Holy Spirit, returned from the Jordan, and was led by the Spirit for forty days in the wilderness, tempted by the devil. And when the devil had ended every temptation, he departed from him until an opportune time. And Jesus returned in the power of the Spirit into Galilee.

And because thou wast acceptable to God, it was necessary that temptation should prove thee.

- John 4:1-2, 13-14, Tobias 12:13

Before proclaiming the kingdom, Jesus underwent temptation in the desert. His temptation began shortly after being baptized by John. "Anyone who contemplates Christ through the various stages of his life cannot fail to perceive in him the truth about man."[8]

The cycle of our spiritual life is seen in these three events; conversion, temptation, and proclamation. Whenever I accept Christ into my life or make a new commitment to Jesus I am almost always immediately led into temptation. Only after suffering through temptation, like Christ, can I effectively proclaim the kingdom of God. As a believer, I am subject to extreme temptations in today's world. No matter where I find my workplace it is filled with temptations because nothing is sacred or off limits to the devil. In the office I may be tempted to lust for the person in the cubicle next to me. On the jobsite I may be tempted to take material that belongs to the company. If my workplace is in the home I may be tempted to neglect my duties or find an easy way out of the task at hand. In all of my work I am tempted to follow the devil to a high place, a place of selfishness. Only when I tell Satan that I adore God alone and will serve only Him will he depart from me. Then I can tell the world that the kingdom of God is at hand.

Our Father, Hail Mary, Glory Be, Etc.
Additional clause: of thy womb, Jesus,

who proclaimed the Kingdom and forgave sins.

The Transfiguration

And after six days Jesus took Peter and James and John his brother, and led them up a high mountain apart. And he was transfigured before them, and his face shone like the sun, and his garments became white as light. And behold there appeared to them Moses and Elijah, talking with him.

He shone in his days as the morning star in the midst of a cloud, and as the moon at the full. And as the sun when it shineth, so did he shine in the temple of God.

- Matthew 17:1-3, Sirach 50:6-7

In the Transfiguration, Jesus reveals Himself. He shows His glory. "Christ the new Adam, in the very revelation of the mystery of the Father and of His love, fully reveals man to man himself and brings to light his most high calling."[9]

I am to imitate Christ in all things and I too am to be transfigured. By studying the "law", represented by Moses, and the prophets, represented by Elijah, and the life of Christ revealed in them I will be changed. The workplace desperately needs to see Christ. By following Christ to the barren desert or to the highest mountain I will be transformed in His image and likeness. Only by following Him anywhere and everywhere He leads me can I experience what Peter, James, and John experienced. I should also spend more time in Eucharistic Adoration so that when co-workers look at me they will see my face shining like the Son!

Our Father, Hail Mary, Glory Be, Etc.
Additional clause:...of thy womb, Jesus,
who was transfigured on Mt. Tabor.

The Institution of the Eucharist

"Where will you have us go and prepare for you to eat the Passover?" And he sent two of his disciples, and said to them, "Go into the city and a man carrying a jar of water will meet you; follow him, and wherever he enters say to the householder, "The Teacher says, where is my guest room... And he will show you a large upper room furnished and ready; there prepare for us."

My son, do thy works in meekness, and thou shalt be beloved above the glory of men.

- Mark 14:12-15, Sirach 3:19

All too often I feel that I am getting nowhere. I feel that everything I do day-by-day amounts to nothing. My life can appear to be an endless cycle of work and sleep. However, I must remember that I have a job to do and that job, no matter how seemingly insignificant, can help further the kingdom.

To the disciples who went to prepare a place for the Passover it may have seemed like just another task given by Our Lord. However, by their obedience to that task, the Eucharist was given to us by Jesus.

God does not ask for great things from me. He only asks me to do ordinary things with great love. If I complete my work with great love, Jesus can use that task to give himself to others. If I tighten the bolt, change the diaper, enter the data, rescue those in danger, or set the table with great love, Jesus can turn that work into a living sign of Himself like the Eucharist. It is with a great desire that He has desired to share my work.

Our Father, Hail Mary, Glory Be, Etc.
Additional clause: ...of thy womb, Jesus,
who gave me Himself in the Eucharist.

The Sorrowful Mysteries of Work

The Agony in the Garden

And being in agony he prayed more earnestly; and his sweat became like great drops of blood falling to the ground.

And the Lord God took man, and put him into the paradise of pleasure, to dress it, and to keep it. And to Adam he said: Because thou hast hearkened to the voice of thy wife, and hast eaten of the tree, whereof I commanded thee, that thou shouldst not eat, cursed is the earth in thy work: with labour and toil shalt thou eat thereof all the days of thy life.

- Luke 22:44, Genesis 2:15, 3:17

Your agony in the garden, Lord, was a work of love. You saw the work ahead of You, the cup You had to drink, and You began to sweat, even to the point of sweating blood. I am reminded of the beginning of this story in an ancient garden. You commanded that man work the garden, but when he disobeyed, You saw fit that he must earn his keep by the sweat of his brow.

Work is a gift from You. No matter how hard, boring, or tedious, I can offer my work and my sweat back to You. Work can be my way to salvation if only I too accept the cup You will have me drink.

Our Father, Hail Mary, Glory Be, Etc.
Additional clause: ...of thy womb, Jesus,
who sweat blood for me.

The Scourging at the Pillar

So Pilate, wishing to satisfy the crowd, released for them Barabbas; and having scourged Jesus, he delivered him to be crucified.

O Lord, thou knowest, remember me, and visit me, and defend me from them that persecute me, do not defend me in thy patience: know that for thy sake I have suffered reproach.

- Mark 15:15, Jeremiah 15:15

You told Peter that "the spirit is willing but the flesh is weak."[10] To atone for my weak flesh, Yours was torn from Your body during the cruel scourging. The work of Your passion continued with each lash of the whip. Like the whip of a task master upon Your back my sins scarred You for eternity.

Many times I too feel the whip of the slave driver. Deadlines, profit, and personal vengeance can slash my back and my soul if I let them. Help me to follow Your example of love given at the pillar. Help me to endure - in Your name for my salvation and for the salvation of those in charge of me - all my difficult and sometimes seemingly impossible situations at work.

Our Father, Hail Mary, Glory Be, Etc.
Additional clause: ...of thy womb, Jesus,
who was scourged for me.

16

The Crowning with Thorns

And they clothed him in a purple cloak, and plaiting a crown of thorns they put it on him. And they began to salute him, "Hail, King of the Jews." And they struck his head with a reed, and spat upon him, and they knelt down in homage to him.

They surrounded me like bees, and they burned like fire among thorns: and in the name of the Lord I was revenged on them. Being pushed I was overturned that I might fall: but the Lord supported me. The Lord is my strength and my praise: and he is become my salvation.

- Mark 15:17-19, Psalm 117:12-14

With a crown of thorns and a purple robe the court jeered and ridiculed You. With patient endurance You continued the work of my salvation. How cruel men can be to their fellow man.

Many times in my own work I want to take off the crown of thorns and robe that I wear. I want to deny my kingship that You earned with Your blood so that I will no longer be jeered, ridiculed, and spat upon with unkind words and slander. It is difficult being a follower of Yours in this world, especially in the work place. Help me to accept the mockery of those I work with who do not believe, and, like You, help me to pray for their forgiveness, "for they know not what they do".[11]

Our Father, Hail Mary, Glory Be, Etc.
Additional clause: … of thy womb, Jesus,
who was crowned with thorns for me.

The Carrying of the Cross

So they took Jesus, and he went out, bearing his own cross, to the place called the place of the skull, which is called in Hebrew Golgotha. And as they led him away, they seized one Simon of Cyrene...and laid on him the cross to carry it behind Jesus.

Even to your old age I am the same, and to your grey hairs I will carry you: I have made you, and I will bear: I will carry and will save.

- John 19:17, Luke 23:26, Isaiah 46:4

Jesus, You said unless I pick up my cross daily and follow You I could not be Your disciple. Isn't it enough to go through what I have already been through? Why this? Why more work, Jesus?

You took up the cross and placed it on Your back like a yoke and carried it to Calvary. You plowed the fallow ground with the cross and planted the seeds of Your blood along the way. How often I refuse to give more. How often I say "enough" to the demands of my time, talent, and treasure. You never said "enough". You instead said, "this is my body which will be given up for you".[12]

Lord help me to give myself totally in all I do, especially my work. Help me to take up my own cross and follow You, and when I am asked to walk a mile with that cross, help me to walk two.

Our Father, Hail Mary, Glory Be, Etc.
Additional clause: ... of thy womb, Jesus,
who bore the heavy cross for me.

The Crucifixion and Death

And when they had crucified him, they divided his garments among them by casting lots; then they sat down and kept watch over him there. And Jesus cried again with a loud voice and yielded up his spirit.

- Matthew 27: 35-36, 50

"How ironic", one might say, the carpenter's hands pierced by nails, nailed to His wood.

Your work was to do the will of the Father no matter the cost, "becoming obedient unto death, even to the death of a cross."[13] My work too is to do the Father's will. In my daily routine I am to follow His commands. There can be great salvific value in my work if I simply offer my every working moment as a sacrifice to God. Many souls can be saved if I work with great love, "for love covers a multitude of sins."[14] In my work, I can pray without ceasing and die daily to myself and my own will. Through my acceptance of the work God commissions me to do, I will indeed, "…work out my salvation with fear and trembling."[15]

Our Father, Hail Mary, Glory Be, Etc.
Additional clause: ..of thy womb, Jesus,
who died for my sins on the Cross.

The Glorious Mysteries of Work

The Resurrection

"He is not here; for he has risen, as he said. Come see the place where he lay. Then go quickly and tell his disciples that he has risen from the dead, and behold he is going before you...you will see him..."

And when he was at the last gasp, he said thus: Thou indeed, O most wicked man, destroyest us out of this present life: but the King of the world will raise us up, who die for his laws, in the resurrection of eternal life.

- Matthew 28: 6-7, 2 Maccabees 7:9

To meditate on work and the Resurrection seems wrong. The Resurrection was on a Sunday and Sunday is a day of rest. This can be seen in the events of Easter Sunday. The Roman guards were relieved of their duty by angels. Our Lord resembled a gardener to Mary Magdalene. Everyone was spared the trouble of rolling back the stone. Sunday is a day of rest. It is a time to put down my burdens and rejoice and be glad. It is a day to spend with the Lord and my family. Work can wait on Sunday. I will rejoice in the glorious gift of Sunday, after all, Sunday was made for man not man for Sunday.

Our Father, Hail Mary, Glory Be, Etc.
Additional clause: of thy womb, Jesus,
who rose from the dead for me.

The Ascension

And while they were gazing into heaven as he went, behold, two men stood by them in white robes, and said, "Men of Galilee, why do you stand looking into heaven? This Jesus, who was taken up from you into heaven, will come in the same way as you saw him go into heaven."

Wherefore be you also ready, because at what hour you know not the Son of man will come. Who, thinkest thou, is a faithful and wise servant, whom his lord hath appointed over his family, to give them meat in season. Blessed is that servant, whom when his lord shall come he shall find so doing.

- Acts of the Apostles 1:10-11, Matthew 24:44-46

"Why are you standing looking up?" The angels remind me that I have a task, I have work to do. They tell me that He will return in a like manner as He left. Jesus asked if He would find faith when He returns. To make disciples of all nations is my commission.

Whether I am doing dishes, data entry, construction, gardening, or piece-work makes no difference. I am not to stand idle watching the skies because I do not know when He will return. The Ascension says to me, "rejoice for He goes to prepare a place for you," but also that I must get to work for He will return and demand an account for every moment of my life.

Our Father, Hail Mary, Glory Be, Etc.
Additional clause: …of thy womb, Jesus,
who ascended into Heaven.

The Descent of the Holy Spirit

And there appeared to them tongues as of fire, distributed and resting on each one of them. And they were all filled with the Holy Spirit and began to speak in other tongues, as the Spirit gave them utterance. ...the promise is to you and your children and to all that are far off...

So let your light shine before men, that they may see your good works, and glorify your Father who is in heaven.

- Acts of the Apostles 2:3-4, 39, Matthew 5:16

Jesus said, "without me, you can do nothing."[16] I cannot say that after the Ascension the Apostles did nothing because they did pray, but they did not work. There must be both work and prayer, a human aspect and a divine aspect. Not until they received the Holy Spirit did they go about the task given them. They had the Holy Spirit, the Spirit of Christ, and they could do all things through Him who strengthened them.[17]

So very often I sit alone in the upper room of my faith. I have received the gifts of the Spirit through Confirmation but the devil tricks me into not using them. I need to speak out at my work place and live a radical life for Christ. If He is within me there is nothing I cannot do. I must call upon the Holy Spirit to guide me in the things I do and say at work in such a way that all who see or hear me will be amazed and turn to Christ.

Our Father, Hail Mary, Glory Be, Etc.
Additional clause: ...of thy womb, Jesus,
who pours forth the Holy Spirit.

The Assumption of Mary

But the woman was given the two wings of the great eagle
that she might fly from the serpent into the wilderness, to the place
where she is to be nourished for a time, and times, and half a time.
Behold, I come quickly; and my reward is with me, to
render to every man according to his works.

- Revelation 12:14, 22:12

Mary's Assumption is another example, another glimpse at the reward for my work; to be in heaven. My work, especially when done for Christ or done for love of Christ, can seem thankless and endless. Long hours away from my family, years of personal sacrifice, and patient endurance of a God-less atmosphere are often rewarded with a few coins and barely a pat on the back. I must always keep in mind that my reward is not waiting for me here on earth but is in heaven. "Eye hath not seen, nor ear heard, neither hath it entered into the heart of man, what things God hath prepared for them that love him."[18]

Our Father, Hail Mary, Glory Be, Etc.
Additional clause: ...of thy womb, Jesus,
who assumed you into Heaven.

23

The Coronation of Mary

And a great sign appeared in heaven, a woman clothed with the sun, with the moon under her feet, and on her head a crown of twelve stars...

And the king rose to meet her, and bowed down to her; then he sat on his throne, and had a seat brought for the king's mother; and she sat on his right.

- Revelation 12:1, 1 Kings 2:19

This final meditation on work brings me to the royal court of heaven where Jesus my King, and Mary my Queen and Mother welcome me after my life in this valley of tears. The Queen and King of this court are no strangers to work. Both set about the work given them with love for God. Both suffered while working and were rewarded by the world with a sword to their hearts. I should draw comfort from the knowledge that my Queen and King have both walked the path before me. Mary, as a homemaker and mother, and Jesus, as a carpenter and teacher, worked and made their work glorify God. I too can make my work glorify God if I choose to offer it always as a prayer.

Our Father, Hail Mary, Glory Be, Etc.
Additional clause: ...of thy womb, Jesus,
who crowned you Queen of Heaven and Earth.

Mysteries of Children

"Children have nothing of their own; everything belongs to their parents…And your Father always knows very well how to mange the household."

- St. Josemaria Escriva   *The Way # 867*

The Joyful Mysteries of Children

The Annunciation

And the angel said to her, "Do not be afraid, Mary, for you have found favor with God. And behold, you will conceive in your womb and bear a son, and you shall call his name Jesus. He will be great and be called the Son of the Most High..."

The wolf shall dwell with the lamb: and the leopard shall lie down with the kid: the calf and the lion, and the sheep shall abide together, and a little child shall lead them.

- Luke 1:31-32, Isaiah 11:6

Children are a gift from God. A completely mysterious gift, but a gift nonetheless. The mystery of the Annunciation shows me how much God loves human life. My salvation did not begin with a celestial light show or trumpeted announcement throughout the heavens. It began with a pregnancy. The Word truly became flesh and entered the world the way I did. My God chose to become a helpless child in the arms of His Mother. For a while the Creator was nurtured at the breast of one of His creatures.

Unless I become like a little child I cannot enter the kingdom.[19] To be child-like is to be full of awe and wonder at everything God does. Small children are amazed at simple things like music, balloons, and bugs. I too need to look at life with that kind of awe. Children are a gift from God because they can teach me how God wants me to live, depending solely on Him and looking with wonder at all He does for me. Like the angel Gabriel children can be messengers from God.

Our Father, Hail Mary, Glory Be, Etc.
Additional clause: ...of thy womb, Jesus,
who was conceived by the Holy Spirit.

The Visitation

"And why is this granted to me, that the mother of my Lord should come to me? For behold, when the voice of your greeting came to my ears, the babe in my womb danced for joy."

And when the ark of the Lord was come into the city of David, Michol the daughter of Saul, looking out through a window, saw king David leaping and dancing before the Lord: and she despised him in her heart.

- *Luke 1:43-44, 2 Samuel 6:16*

I often wonder whether the Visitation was for Mary to visit Elizabeth or for Jesus to visit John. Watching children play can be a delightful experience. Their unchecked enthusiasm is beautiful in itself. How often adults subdue their love and zeal for life and each other out of pride. I often fear what people may say if they see me get really excited about anything. If I truly love God this sort of pride and fear should not exist. Not only did John leap unashamedly in his mother's womb, his mother was equally exuberant upon seeing her cousin. It is time that I become like a little child and truly allow myself to get excited and rejoice in others. I need to meet and greet my neighbors with child-like abandonment and leap with joy in my heart like John, cry out blessings like Elizabeth, and proclaim the greatness of God like Mary.

Our Father, Hail Mary, Glory Be, Etc.
Additional clause: ...of thy womb, Jesus,
whom you carried to Elizabeth.

The Nativity

...and going into the house they saw the child with Mary his mother, and they fell down and worshipped him. Then, opening their treasures, they offered him gifts, gold and frankincense and myrrh.

Be not solicitous therefore, saying, What shall we eat: or what shall we drink, or wherewith shall we be clothed? For after all these things do the heathens seek. For your Father knoweth that you have need of all these things. Seek ye therefore first the kingdom of God, and his justice, and all these things shall be added unto you.

- Matthew 2:11, 6:31-33

Having many things or objects does not make people happy. In today's society the one-with-the-most-toys-wins mentality prevails. Jesus was born into poverty but He did not want because He had the love of His Mother and the example and protection of His adoptive father. Children do not need things to make them happy. They do not need toys or computer games. They need parents who will love, teach, and protect them. No amount of money or number of goods will make any child happy and holy. Only love, sacrifice, good example, and protection can ensure that. Jesus was given gold, frankincense, and myrrh as symbolic gifts. Like many parents, Mary and Joseph probably saw them as nothing more than Christmas presents to store in the basement or give away in a few years. I need to stop giving my children so many gifts and start giving them God.

Our Father, Hail Mary, Glory Be, Etc.
Additional clause: ...of thy womb, Jesus,
who was born in Bethlehem.

The Presentation in the Temple

"Behold this child is set for the fall and rising of many in Israel, and a for a sign that is spoken against (and a sword will pierce through your own soul also) that thoughts out of many hearts may be revealed."

The rich have wanted, and have suffered hunger: but they that seek the Lord shall not be deprived of any good. Come, children, hearken to me: I will teach you the fear of the Lord.

- Luke 2:34-35, Psalm 33:11-12

Children are a tremendous responsibility. Not only do they need to be fed, taught, cared for and protected, they also need to reared in the Faith and given back to God. During the Baptismal Rite children are given a white gown symbolic of the newness and holiness of their soul now cleansed of original sin. Parents and godparents for their part, promise to raise them according to the teachings of the Church. They also promise to help them return to God with their souls as clean as they are at the moment of Baptism.

Mary offered Jesus back to God without reservation. Her gift of her Son enabled His gift of Himself to me. How often do I try to control my children instead of leading them? How often do I put my own fears and anxieties on them?

Lord, help me to offer my children to You without reservation and no matter the cost even if a sword must pierce my heart as well.

Our Father, Hail Mary, Glory Be, Etc.
Additional clause: ...of thy womb, Jesus,
whom you presented in the Temple.

The Finding of Jesus in the Temple

...and when they did not find him, they returned to Jerusalem, seeking him. After three days they found him in the temple, sitting among the teachers, listening to them, and asking them questions.

And the father said to his servants: Bring forth quickly the first robe, and put it on him, and put a ring on his hand, and shoes on his feet: And bring hither the fatted calf, and kill it, and let us eat and make merry: Because this my son was dead, and is come to life again: was lost, and is found. And they began to be merry.

- Luke 2:45-46, 15:22-24

Losing my keys or wallet is one thing, but losing a child is completely different. Any parent who has simply lost sight of his or her child for a few unexpected moments knows the heart wrenching feelings that accompany that loss. Many parents have lost their children to accidents, crimes, or suicides. Many others feel the same loss with children who have run away, become addicted, or left the Faith.

Mary felt the agony of loss when she realized Jesus wasn't to be found. She felt the agony of loss, but she was not overcome by it. Her hope remained strong.

Lord, help me to always hold on to hope. Help me to trust You even when I feel that I have lost You or You have left me. Give hope to those parents who are experiencing a difficult time with their children, especially those experiencing loss. Help them to turn to Your Mother for comfort. Mother of Hope, pray for us.

Our Father, Hail Mary, Glory Be, Etc.
Additional clause: ...of thy womb, Jesus,
whom you found in the Temple.

The Luminous Mysteries of Children

The Baptism of Our Lord

"Even now the axe is laid to the root of the trees,; every tree therefore that does not bear good fruit is cut down and thrown into the fire. I baptize you with water for repentance, but he who is coming after me is mightier than I, whose sandals I am not worthy to carry..."

Hear, ye children, the instruction of a father, and attend, that you may know prudence. I will give you a good gift, forsake not my law. For I also was my father's son, tender, and as an only son in the sight of my mother: And he taught me, and said: Let thy heart receive my words, keep my commandments, and thou shalt live.

- Matthew 3:10-11, Proverbs 4:1-4

John the Baptist is the perfect example of what can happen when children are exposed early to Christ. Through the grace of the Visitation John becomes the "voice" crying out in the wilderness. John knows his place. He knows he is the messenger not the Message. He knows he is not even fit to loosen Jesus' sandal strap. John also knows that he must decrease so that Christ may increase. Like St. Paul, John is to say, "It is no longer I that live but Christ that lives in me."[20]

To help create a "culture of life", I must raise up sons and daughters to be like John. I must teach them by my example to be voices crying out in the wilderness of this world. It is only possible to set this example when I decrease so that Christ might increase in me. Then and only then will I hear a voice say to me and my children, "you are my beloved in whom I am well pleased."

Our Father, Hail Mary, Glory Be, Etc.
Additional clause: ...of thy womb, Jesus,

31

who was baptized by John.

The Wedding at Cana

*When the wine failed, the mother of Jesus said to him,
"they have no wine." And Jesus said to her, "O woman what is
this to me and to thee? My hour has not yet come."*

*For whereas he had always feared God from his infancy,
and kept his commandments, he repined not against God because
the evil of blindness had befallen him, But continued immoveable
in the fear of God, giving thanks to God all the days of his life.*

- John 2:3-4, Tobias 2:13-14

"What is this to me and to thee?" With these words Jesus reminds
his Mother that whatever happens to Him will affect her. He
subtly reminds her of the prophecy of Simeon, "And thy own soul
a sword shall pierce, that, out of many hearts, thoughts may be
revealed."[21]

As a parent my heart is pierced many times. I suffer both with and
because of my children. Mary knew that this miracle would begin
her suffering but she asked Him to do it anyway because of the
love she has for us, her adopted children. Suffering is an
unavoidable experience for parents. Yet when I am suffering with
or because of my children I have a great opportunity to save souls
by turning more fully to God. Parents must both follow and echo
Mary's words and tell our children to "do whatever he tells you."[22]

Our Father, Hail Mary, Glory Be, Etc.
Additional clause: …of thy womb, Jesus,
who transformed water into wine.

The Proclamation of the Kingdom

"See that you do not despise one of these little ones; for I tell you that in heaven their angels always behold the face of my Father who is in heaven." ...but Jesus said to them, "Let the children come to me, and do not hinder them; for to such belongs the kingdom of heaven."

Ye that fear the Lord, love him, and your hearts shall be enlightened. My children behold the generations of men: and know ye that no one hath hoped in the Lord, and hath been confounded. For who hath continued in his commandment, and hath been forsaken? or who hath called upon him, and he despised him?

- Matthew 18:10, 19:14, Sirach 2:10-12

"(T)he kingdom of God is at hand; repent, and believe the Gospel."[23] With these words Jesus begins His ministry. Jesus tells us that the world was about to change and forever be changed. He goes on to call all men to holiness through Himself.

When a child comes into our life, our world changes. From that point on nothing ever stays the same and the whole history of the human race is changed. Man is made in the image and likeness of God. This is readily apparent in the face of the young. I must hear the words of Christ as I hold my children in my arms. The kingdom is present within these precious gifts. In order for me to proclaim the kingdom to my children I must repent and believe the Gospel. I must repent of my selfishness, anger, and pride. I must believe in the Gospel and the truth that Jesus calls me and them to be with Him in paradise. When I read the Gospel, I should believe what I read, preach what I believe, and practice what I preach.

Our Father, Hail Mary, Glory Be, Etc.
Additional clause: ...of thy womb, Jesus,
who proclaimed the Kingdom and forgave sins.

The Transfiguration

And he was transfigured before them and his face shone like the sun, and his garments became white as light. And Peter said to Jesus, "Lord, it is well that we are here; if you wish, I will make three booths here, one for you and one for Moses and one for Elijah."

That which was from the beginning, which we have heard, which we have seen with our eyes, which we have looked upon, and our hands have handled, of the word of life: That which we have seen and have heard, we declare unto you, that you also may have fellowship with us, and our fellowship may be with the Father, and with his Son Jesus Christ.

- Matthew 17:2,4, 1 John 1:1,3

"Out of the mouths of babes" so the saying goes. One of the most beautiful qualities of children is that they speak their minds. They do not hide emotions. They are open and honest about their feelings. During the transfiguration Peter is like a child. In his excitement he blurts out what on the surface seems like a silly statement. But it is not silly for those with childlike faith. Peter, like many children, was so caught up in what was happening he did not want it to end. He is like a child who never wants to come off the merry-go-round. Peter saw Christ for who He was and did not want things to go back to normal. When I reach the point where I see Christ for who He truly is, God, I will also be transfigured. I will not want to come off the beautiful ride of faith.

Lord, help me to not look at You in a generic way as friend or brother. Help me to see You with childlike faith, transfigured and radiant as Lord and Savior. Then, I too will never want to leave Your side.

Our Father, Hail Mary, Glory Be, Etc.
Additional clause: ...of thy womb, Jesus,
who was transfigured on Mt. Tabor.

35

The Institution of the Eucharist

And he took bread, and when he had given thanks he broke it and gave it to them, saying, "This is my body which is given up for you. Do this in remembrance of me." And likewise the cup after supper, saying, "This cup which is poured out for you is the new covenant in my blood." A dispute arose among them, which of them was to be regarded as the greatest.

For we are the children of the saints, and look for that life which God will give to those that never change their faith from him.

- Luke 22:19-20, 24, Tobit 2:18

There is a great difference between having childlike faith and being childish. My children have faith that I will hold them, feed them, and protect them. They do not ponder the reason why I would do this; they simply have faith. However, they become childish when they are jealous of each other assuming I love one more than the other.

The disciples acted in much the same way in Luke's Gospel. With childlike faith they believe Jesus when He says, "this is my body, this is my blood". Immediately afterwards a debate ensues over who is the greatest or who is loved more.

My children must be taught that faith is a gift freely given to us from God the Father through the Son. I must protect them from those who would try to take their faith. I should feed them with both the Word, as in Scripture, and the Word made flesh, Jesus in the Eucharist. I must teach them that we are all loved by God equally, from the worst sinner to the greatest saint. I must teach them not to be concerned with the gifts God has given others but with their own gifts and how to use them to give Him glory.

Our Father, Hail Mary, Glory Be, Etc.
Additional clause: …of thy womb, Jesus,
who gives me His Body and Blood in the Eucharist.

36

The Sorrowful Mysteries of Children

The Agony in the Garden

Then he said to them, "My soul is very sorrowful, even unto death; remain here, and watch with me." And going a little further he fell on his face and prayed, "My Father, if it be possible, let this cup pass from me; nevertheless, not as I will, but as thou wilt."

O Lord, who hast the holy knowledge, thou knowest manifestly that whereas I might be delivered from death, I suffer grievous pains in body: but in soul am well content to suffer these things, because I fear thee.

- Matthew 26:28-39, 2 Maccabees 6:30

Christ sweat blood in the garden because of my sins. He was in agony over what He was to suffer for my sake. He loved me so much and knew I couldn't pay the price so He took my place and punishment.

When my child suffers I feel the agony of Christ. Colds, fevers, the flu, and broken bones or cuts keep parents up all night agonizing over their children wishing they could take the pain away. Multiple sclerosis, leukemia, and cancer bring many parents to their knees and often to the point of sweating drops of blood in agony over the suffering of their children. I am only human and no amount of promises can take away the suffering my children may experience. Only God can heal the sick but my prayers and petitions can bring about that healing. In my own agony, bedside them on my knees, I can accept this cup of suffering for the salvation of my children and the world. "But not what I will, but what thou wilt."[24]

Our Father, Hail Mary, Glory Be, Etc.
Additional clause: ...of thy womb, Jesus,
who sweat blood for me.

The Scourging at the Pillar

*...and having scourged Jesus, delivered him to be crucified.
Then the soldiers of the governor took Jesus into the praetorian,
and they gathered the whole battalion before him.*

*But I am a worm and no man; scorned by men, and
despised by the people.*

- Matthew 27:26-27, Psalm 22:6

Our Lord was cruelly scourged at the pillar by men who were someone's sons. These men were once children themselves. Cruel children can grow up to be cruel men. Often, children can be cold and cruel to each other. Snide remarks about physical deformities, skin color or beliefs fill the playgrounds and homes of cruel families. I must remember to pray for those children who are living in a cruel world. I must also pray for the wisdom to give good example to my own children. Most importantly I must teach my children to imitate Christ and pray for those who scourge them with their lips and whose sharp tongues slice into their backs.

Our Father, Hail Mary, Glory Be, Etc.
Additional clause: ...of thy womb, Jesus,
who was scourged for my offenses.

The Crowning with Thorns

And they stripped him and put a scarlet robe upon him, and plaiting a crown of thorns they put it on his head, and put a reed in his right hand. And kneeling before him they mocked him saying, "Hail, King of the Jews!"

All who see me mock at me, they make mouths at me, they wag their heads...

- Matthew 27:28-29, Psalm 22:7

"He that spareth the rod, hateth his son: but he that loveth him, correcteth him betimes."[25] In today's world, loving discipline seems to be non-existent. The media is filled with horror stories of children who have turned on their parents. The world cannot understand the problem. "The parents gave them everything," they say, "they seemed normal to us". Parents are often tempted to be lenient towards their children. They are told that if they are too strict or try to enforce rules, the child's self-esteem will be damaged. However, the end result is the destruction of the person they were created to be. As in most cases, the world has everything reversed.

God is the sculptor but He allows us, as parents, to swing the hammer. If we do not imitate God the Father with firm and loving discipline, the beautiful sculpting of our children will not take place. "For whom the Lord loveth, he chastiseth."[26] Even though discipline can be difficult and painful, without discipline our crown of royalty won by Christ becomes a crown of thorns.

Lord, give me the wisdom and guidance to lead my children to the crown of victory over sin and self for love of You. Help me to guide them away from the false crown of pride and mockery of God. Give them the grace to accept discipline and see that it is a sign of true love.

Our Father, Hail Mary, Glory Be, Etc.
Additional clause: ...of thy womb, Jesus,
who was crowned with thorns for me.

39

The Carrying of the Cross

So they took Jesus, and he went out, bearing his own cross, to the place called the place of a skull, which is called in Hebrew Golgotha.

...and the Lord has laid on him the iniquity of us all.

- John 19:17, Isaiah 53:6

Jesus had to carry the cross of my sins because He is the Savior. He is the only one who could carry that cross. Often times I want to trade in my cross for a lighter, smaller one.

To raise my children according to the Gospel I must teach them to take up their cross daily. I must teach them that only they can carry the cross given to them and they should never want to lay it down or give up when they fall under its weight. To be Christ-like is to carry my cross out of love for others and also to allow others to help me with my cross. Whether my cross is a physical, mental, or spiritual one makes no difference. It was made for me. If it is rubbing me the wrong way it may be because I have not embraced it tightly enough. I must teach my children to embrace their cross daily and dearly.

Lord, help me to teach my children to accept their cross. Help me to help them with their cross and give me the humility to allow them to help me with my cross. We are Christ and cross for each other.

Our Father, Hail Mary, Glory Be, Etc.
Additional clause: ...of thy womb, Jesus,
who carried the cross for me.

The Crucifixion and Death

When Jesus saw his mother, and the disciple whom he loved standing near, he said to his mother, "Woman, behold your son!" Then he said to the disciple, "Behold, your mother!" And from that hour the disciple took her to his own home.

Let no one despise your youth, but set the believers an example in speech and conduct, in love, in faith, in purity.

- John 19:26-27, 1 Timothy 4:12

The teenage years can be a time of great suffering. Peer pressure, schoolwork, wanting to fit in, trying to be cool while still loving your family, can all weigh heavily on teens. How fitting it is that the one person closest to Our Lord was a teen. John was a mere teenager yet he was present at the Crucifixion when the "men" had run away. It takes great strength to go through the teen years. It took great strength to witness the Crucifixion of Christ. Like John, teens also witness a crucifixion and death but it is of themselves. An intense suffering comes when they must crucify their childish ways and die to themselves.

But like John, they are not alone. "Behold thy Mother!" To imitate Christ and Mary to my teens means to sacrifice my life that they might have "life and have it more abundantly". It also means simply being there to listen and to comfort. If I imitate Christ and Mary, my teens will imitate John and not need any special instructions. They will from that hour take the faith into their own home and their own hearts.

Our Father, Hail Mary, Glory Be, Etc.
Additional clause: …of thy womb, Jesus,
who was crucified for me.

41

The Glorious Mysteries of Children

The Resurrection

...he said to them, "Why do you make a tumult and weep?
The child is not dead but sleeping." And they laughed at him. But
he put them all outside, and took the child's father and mother and
those who were with him, and went in where the child was. Taking
her by the hand he said to her, "Talitha cumi"; which means,
"Little girl, I say to you, arise "...

(she) beheld her seven sons slain in the space of one day,
and bore it with a good courage, for the hope that she had in God.

- Mark 5:39-41 (RSV), 2 Maccabees 7:20

How fitting it is that the first person in the Gospel Jesus raises
from the dead is a child. Shortly after, Jesus tells His followers
that if they love their mother or father, son or daughter more than
Him, they are not worthy of Him.[27] The father must have loved his
daughter dearly to have risked approaching Jesus and paying Him
homage.

Many parents would gladly do anything to bring their children
back from the dead, back from an addiction, or back to the Faith. I
am to love my children but not more than I love Christ. Many
saints have watched their children brutally murdered because of
the Faith. They were able to do this and I can too if I love Christ
and trust that I will hear him say, "little girl, little boy arise!"

Our Father, Hail Mary, Glory Be, Etc.
Additional clause: ... of thy womb, Jesus,
who will rescue me from death

The Ascension

And when he had said this, as they were looking on, he was lifted up, and a cloud took him out of their sight.

Return, O Lord, how long? and be entreated in favour of thy servants.

- Acts of the Apostles 1:9, Psalm 89:13

I often see children looking steadfastly toward heaven as a plane flies overhead. Other times they stare at a kite or a balloon which has escaped their grip. They watch in awe as it floats heavenward. Amazed and saddened they watch intently wishing they could bring it back.

I too wish for Christ to come back. I am amazed at the thought of Him ascending into heaven and saddened that I no longer have Him at hand. Jesus said He would be with us "even til the end of the age."[28] He is with us in the Eucharist and in each believer. Unlike a child's balloon, Jesus will return in the same manner that He left. I must be ready and look for His return as I walk this earth with childlike faith and wonder. I must also teach my children to always be alert and ready for His return.

Our Father, Hail Mary, Glory Be, Etc.
Additional clause: ...of thy womb, Jesus,
who ascended into heaven.

43

The Descent of the Holy Spirit

And at this sound the multitude came together, and they were bewildered, because each one heard them speaking in their own language. And they were amazed and wondered, saying, "Are not all these who are speaking Galileans? And how is it that we hear, each of us in his own language?"

If I speak with the tongues of men, and of angels, and have not charity, I am become as sounding brass, or a tinkling cymbal. And if I should have prophecy and should know all mysteries, and all knowledge, and if I should have all faith, so that I could remove mountains, and have not charity, I am nothing

- Acts of the Apostles 2:7-8, 1 Corinthians 13:1-2

All children regardless of race, color, sex, or creed know one language. It is the language of love. The more they are surrounded by it the more they use it. The outpouring of the Holy Spirit on Pentecost was an outpouring of love. God poured His love on His children in great abundance.

The best way to learn a new language is immersion. To learn the language of Pentecost I must gather my heart into the upper room of my soul and immerse myself in God's love. At Confirmation I was given the full outpouring of the Holy Spirit, a full outpouring of Love. The language of love is a language everyone can understand, but not one that everyone can speak.

Lord, help me to learn this language and all of its dialects. Help me teach my children so that they may be able to communicate with all Your children.

Our Father, Hail Mary, Glory Be, Etc.
Additional clause: ...of thy womb, Jesus,
pouring forth his Holy Spirit.

The Assumption of Mary

*But the woman was given the two wings of the great eagle
that she might fly from the serpent into the wilderness, to the place
where she is to be nourished for a time, and times, and half a time.*
*And the king shall greatly desire thy beauty; for he is the
Lord thy God, and him they shall adore.*

- Revelation 12:14, Psalm 44:12

"The woman was given two wings of a great eagle that she might
fly to the wilderness to her place." I must not forget that Mary too
is a child of God. She was not much more than a child when she
received her calling to be the Mother of God. My children too can
receive their calling from God early, if I do not hinder it. I must
support my children and nurture their dreams. Even dreams can be
an instrument of God. I must love and protect my children, but I
must let go of them so that God may lift them to lofty positions as
He did for Mary. Raising my children in the Faith makes them
humble before God and allows them to be lifted up so that they
may proclaim the greatness of the Lord. "He hath put down the
mighty from their seat, and hath exalted the humble."[29]

Our Father, Hail Mary, Glory Be, Etc.
Additional clause: ...of thy womb, Jesus,
who assumed you into heaven.

45

The Coronation of Mary

And a great sign appeared in heaven, a woman clothed with the sun, with the moon under her feet, and on her head a crown of twelve stars

...And the king rose to meet her, and bowed down to her; then he sat on his throne, and had a seat brought for the king's mother; and she sat on his right.

- Revelation 12:1, 1 Kings 2:19

"He went to make war with the rest of her offspring."[30] The thought of children at war is horrifying, yet a war is what I am in the midst of as a Christian. The battle that the children of God and the children of Mary face has many fronts. I must do battle with the spirit of the world which denies Christ and prides self. I must do battle with flesh which is constantly at odds with my spirit. Finally, I must do battle with the devil himself. He is both my tempter and accuser.

The war between good and evil, light and dark, has been won but the battles rage on. I must train the future fighters, my children, in the ways of spiritual warfare. I must teach my children, God's children, the beauty of creation, the strength of the spirit, and the fear of God to counteract the three constant battles. I must also teach them about the Kingdom for which we fight, and its King and Queen.

Queen of the angels and saints, heaven and earth, wrap your children and my children in your mantle. Mary, Queen of Heaven and Earth, pray for us.

Our Father, Hail Mary, Glory Be, Etc.
Additional clause: ..of thy womb, Jesus,
who crowned you Queen of Heaven

Mysteries of Death

"Haven't you heard the mournful tone with which the worldly complain that "each day that passes is a step nearer to death"?

It is. And I tell you: rejoice, apostolic soul, for each day that passes brings you closer to life."

- St. Josemaria Escriva   The Way # 737

The Joyful Mysteries of Death

The Annunciation

...the angel Gabriel was sent from God to a city of Galilee named Nazareth, to a virgin betrothed to a man whose name was Joseph, of the house of David; and the virgin's name was Mary.

And when I had seen him, I fell at his feet as dead. And he laid his right hand upon me, saying: Fear not. I am the First and the Last, And alive, and was dead, and behold I am living for ever and ever, and have the keys of death and of hell.

- Luke 1:26-27, Revelation 1:17-18

It seems strange to meditate on death as associated with the Joyful Mysteries of the rosary. Yet to meditate on death is a spiritually healthy thing to do. I, like Jesus, from the moment of conception am moving towards death. Death is as natural as life, yet I fear it because it is a realm unknown to me. As the Catechism states, my purpose is to "know, love, and serve God in this life so I can be happy with Him in the next."[31] This very statement has the shadow of death behind it. In reality, death is a prerequisite for eternal life. If I remember death daily, I will be strong enough to say with Mary, "Be it done unto me according to thy word."[32] "Every man dies, but not every man really lives,"[33] the actor said. By constantly remembering death is only a breath away, I can "really live" for God.

Our Father, Hail Mary, Glory Be, Etc.
Additional clause: ...of thy womb, Jesus,
who was conceived by the Holy Spirit

The Visitation

"And why is this granted to me, that the mother of my Lord should come to me? For behold, when the voice of your greeting came to my ears, the babe in my womb danced for joy."

In all thy works, remember thy last end, and thou shalt never sin.

- Luke 1:43-44, Sirach 7:40

In the Visitation, there is new life as well as death. The one called barren is in her sixth month. The virgin has conceived a child who will be called Emmanuel. One woman is in the spring of her life while the other is entering the winter of hers. Both have been blessed by the Lord with their pregnancies. Yet neither knows to what end their children are heading.

Tomorrow is never certain, yet that gives me no claim to fear. If I am following my call to holiness moment by moment, death cannot take me by surprise. John could have recanted and apologized to Herod but he chose instead to lose his head. Jesus could have saved the human race in any other way but His love was so strong it conquered death. I too must be prepared to take Christ with haste to the world even if it means my death, for as St. Paul says, "O death where art thou sting?"[34]

Our Father, Hail Mary, Glory Be, Etc.
Additional clause: ...of thy womb, Jesus,
who calls me to give my life.

The Nativity

Then Herod perceiving that he was deluded by the wise men, was exceedingly angry; and sending killed all the men children that were in Bethlehem, and in all the borders thereof, from two years old and under

...A voice was heard on high of lamentation, of mourning, and weeping, of Rachel weeping for her children, and refusing to be comforted for them, because they are not.

- Matthew 2:16, Jeremiah 31:15

"This day, is born to you a Savior, who is Christ the Lord, in the city of David."[35] With this message the angels brought glad tidings to the earth to men of good will. However, in the background can be heard the rumbling of death like a tidal wave heading toward Bethlehem. By a king's decree the hunt for the King of Kings had begun, and many died in His place.

My joy can sometimes be overshadowed by another's tragedy. I rejoiced at so many lives being spared in the World Trade Center attacks while others were mourning the death of loved ones. I must not forget to be compassionate toward those who are suffering loss. In my times of joy I should reach out to the widowed and orphaned. The circle of life continues and one day it will be my turn to deal with loss. *Tempis fugit, memento mori-* Time Flies, Remember Death.

Our Father, Hail Mary, Glory Be, Etc.
Additional clause: ...of thy womb, Jesus,
who was born to die for me.

The Presentation

And behold there was a man in Jerusalem named Simeon, and this man was just and devout, waiting for the consolation of Israel; and the Holy Ghost was in him.

I must work the works of him that sent me whist it is still day: the night cometh when no man can work.

- Luke 2:25, John 9:4

Many older people, the ones seemingly closer to death, are very wise. Their life experience has imparted wisdom that only God can give. "Dismiss thy servant, O Lord, according to thy word in peace..."[36] Simeon had certainly seen plenty of life and death. It was revealed to him that he would not see his own death until he saw the Christ. Simeon waited patiently and dutifully for the Lord's promise to be fulfilled. When it was fulfilled he was ready to depart this life.

God has promised eternal life to those who love Him, but only after He is through with them in this life. God is the giver and taker of life. There is no "mercy" in mercy killing. There are two times in man's life when he needs extra care, at birth and at death. I should be compassionate and visit with the sick, elderly, and dying. Maybe through the grace of God they will see Christ in me and say, "I am ready Lord, let your servant go in peace."

Our Father, Hail Mary, Glory Be, Etc.
Additional clause: ...of thy womb, Jesus,
whom Simeon held in his arms.

The Finding in the Temple

And not finding him, they returned into Jerusalem, seeking him. And it came to pass, that, after three days, they found him in the temple, sitting in the midst of the doctors, hearing them, and asking them questions.

I know that thou wilt deliver me to death, where a house is appointed for everyone that liveth.

- Luke 2: 45-46, Job 30:23

In reality, life doesn't always turn out as pleasant as the Finding in the Temple. Every year thousands of people disappear never to be seen again. Death is a part of life. Even at the great time of joy in finding Jesus in the Temple the words of Simeon must have been in the background of Mary's heart.

Death comes to us all and in many cases in unforeseen and tragic ways. When these things happen I am not to lose hope. I am called to be like Mary and search that much harder for God's will. Whether it be three days or one hundred and three years, I am called to seek Christ. Like Mary, if I constantly remember death, I can continue to follow God's will through the agony of loss to the joy of finding Him.

Our Father, Hail Mary, Glory Be, Etc.
Additional clause: ...of thy womb, Jesus,
who teaches me about death.

52

The Luminous Mysteries of Death

The Baptism of Jesus

Behold I will bring the waters of a great flood upon the earth, to destroy all flesh...And she came to him in the evening carrying the bough of an olive tree...he therefore understood that the waters were ceased upon the earth.

And the Holy Ghost descended in a bodily shape, as a dove upon him; and a voice came from heaven: Thou art my beloved Son; in thee I am well pleased.

- Genesis 6:17a, 8:11, Luke 3:22

Baptism is symbolic of death. It is the death of the old man and the rebirth of the new. Through Baptism I am able to experience heaven more fully because I am changed and conformed to Christ. I must die so that Christ may live in me or as John later says, " He must increase, but I must decrease."[37]

Death comes to everyone whether they are ready or not. In Noah's time man's heart was bent toward evil and God had to "baptize" the earth in order for it to be made new. When he was finished, a dove returned to the ark. In Jesus' time, again, man's heart was set on evil. Only this time God chose to smite His Son instead of the entire earth. This was foreshadowed by Christ's baptism and again a dove is seen.

I have no need to fear death for I have already died once, in baptism. "For we are buried together with him by baptism into death."[38] Through this death and rebirth I was born into the Kingdom.

> Our Father, Hail Mary, Glory Be, Etc.
> Additional clause: ...of thy womb, Jesus,
> who has conquered the waters of death.

The Wedding at Cana

*And the third day, there was a marriage in Cana of
Galilee: and the mother of Jesus was there. And Jesus also was
invited, and his disciples, to the marriage.
...in the resurrection they shall neither marry nor be
married; but shall be as the angels of God in heaven.*

- John 2:1-2, Matthew 22:30

A wedding is a strange place to meditate on death. It is meant to
be one of the happiest days of a husband and wife's life. But I
must not forget the vows of marriage; "Until death do us part."
Only death can separate husband and wife, and only death to self
can give life to the marriage.

Death was the farthest thing from my mind during my wedding,
but it should always be in my thoughts. I must also consider that
"the two become one". In this there is new life spiritually and
hopefully physically in children. The two parts that have now
become one are a new creation. If anyone tries to make the one
become two again, neither will survive spiritually for long. This is
a mystery that all married people and engaged people should
meditate upon. Only death can end a marriage. "What therefore
God has joined, let no man put asunder."[39]

Our Father, Hail Mary, Glory Be, Etc.
Additional clause: ...of thy womb, Jesus,
who is Lord of life and death.

The Proclamation of the Kingdom

From that time Jesus began to preach, and to say: Do penance, for the kingdom of heaven is at hand.

Behold, I see the heavens opened, and the Son of man standing on the right hand of God. And they crying out with a loud voice, stopped their ears, and with one accord ran violently upon him. And casting him forth without the city, they stoned him...

- Matthew 4:17, Acts of the Apostles 7:55c-57

In proclaiming the Kingdom Jesus gives me a radical list of ideas to embrace - Turning my cheek, loving my enemy, not being angry with my neighbor and so on. The proclamation of the Kingdom is nothing short of a martyr's marching orders. To follow the beatitudes to the fullest means death, certain death, for Christ's sake. To read about the martyrs is easy. To follow them is extremely difficult. What many of them died for, I seldom consider offensive. Their motto has always been "to die rather than sin". Is this my motto? To proclaim the Kingdom I must follow Christ. He gave His very life for me on the Cross. I too must be ready to die. I must be willing to offer my blood as seed for the harvest of souls. I must be ready to die rather than sin!

Our Father, Hail Mary, Glory Be, Etc.
Additional clause: ...of thy womb, Jesus,
who asks me to lose my life for His sake

The Transfiguration

And he was transfigured before them. And his face did shine as the sun: and his garments became white as snow. And behold there appeared to them Moses and Elias talking with him.
With him that feareth the Lord, it shall go well in the latter end, and in the day of his death he shall be blessed.

- Matthew 17:2-3, Sirach 1:13

The transfiguration of Our Lord offers great hope to me as I am dying. Not only do I see Christ in His glory as though resurrected, but I also see two of my own. Moses and Elijah, who represent the Law and the Prophets, are seen on the mountain speaking with Jesus.

Yes, it is true, I, like everyone else, am dying and I may see death soon, but I must find comfort in the transfiguration. For truly my God is the God of the living and not of the dead. Moses did not enter the earthly promised land, but he did enter the heavenly one. Elijah left this world in a chariot of fire to enter the next. In the transfiguration I have hope in the face of death. If I truly belong to Christ I too, after death, will see the God of the living in the land of the living.

Our Father, Hail Mary, Glory Be, Etc.
Additional clause: ...of thy womb, Jesus,
who was transfigured on Mt. Tabor

The Institution of the Eucharist

*He that eateth my flesh, and drinketh my blood, hath
everlasting life: and I will raise him up in the last day. For my
flesh is meat indeed: and my blood is drink indeed. He that eateth
my flesh, and drinketh my blood, abideth in me, and I in him -
This is my body, which is given for you.*

- John 6:55-57, Luke 22:19

"Except you eat the flesh of the Son of man, and drink his blood,
you shall not have life in you."[40] The death of Jesus was necessary
for me to have eternal life. Jesus says that I cannot have
everlasting life unless I eat His flesh and drink His blood. No life
can come forth in any situation unless there is death. Adam
experienced the "little death" so that Eve might come forth from
his side and bring abundant life. The lives of Joseph's brothers
would not have been saved if he had not been sold into slavery and
thought of as dead.

"And we know that to them that love God, all things work together
unto good."[41] This is true even in death. The apostles did not want
Jesus to be handed over because they could not see the great and
wonderful gift of the Eucharist. They could not see the "source
and summit" of the Christian faith at the Last Supper.

Lord, help me to see Your will in times of loss. Help me to
remember that You have plans for my good and not for evil. Lord,
give me the grace to conform fully to Christ so that when He
returns He will say to me, this now is bone of my bone, flesh of my
flesh, this is my body, this is my blood.

Our Father, Hail Mary, Glory Be, Etc.
Additional clause: ...of thy womb, Jesus,
who gives me life through His flesh.

The Sorrowful Mysteries of Death

The Agony in the Garden

And being in an agony, he prayed the longer. And his sweat became as drops of blood, trickling down upon the ground.

Afflicted in few things, in many they shall be well rewarded: because God hath tried them, and found them worthy of himself.

- Luke 22:43-44, Wisdom 3:5

Jesus was in agony because He knew the type of death He would face. He did not want this to happen but submitted to the Father's will. The agony in the garden involved a great deal of suffering for Jesus even to the point of sweating blood. But the agony of Christ in the garden must also be seen as a time of grace. For many, death comes unexpectedly like a thief in the night. For others death is a long night of agony that can last weeks, months, or years. This time of agony must be seen as a time of grace, a gift from God. It is a chance for conversion, reparation, and time to be with God. The treatments, physical pains, mental anguish, and the disease or injury itself can be a tremendous source of redemptive suffering.

If I too kneel with my cancer, AIDS, or any other terminal illness and say to God, "not my will but Yours be done", I can save souls and make reparation for my past sins. This by no means suggests that my pain will be removed, but it will be united with Christ as I continue with Him toward Calvary.

Our Father, Hail Mary, Glory Be, Etc.
Additional clause: ...of thy womb, Jesus,
who is with me as I face death.

The Scourging at the Pillar

Then therefore, Pilate took Jesus, and scourged him.
But he was wounded for our iniquities, he was bruised for
our sins: the chastisement of our peace was upon him, and by his
bruises we are healed.

- John 19:1, Isaiah 53:5

"I did not find this man guilty...I will therefore chastise Him and release Him."[42] Life can seem so unfair. Pilate's logic was illogical. Punish the innocent? As I travel one step closer to Calvary with Jesus I see that bad things happen to good people. Death can seem so unfair. "Why did God take him?", I might ask. "He had his whole life ahead of him". "I hate seeing her suffer, she doesn't deserve this". Many times death, and the suffering it can bring, seem unfair. An otherwise perfectly healthy father with an inoperable brain tumor. A newborn baby given only days to live. So many examples of innocent suffering and death.

God's ways are not my ways. No matter what the situation or circumstance I must remember that nothing happens that does not pass though His hands. Jesus was found innocent by Pilate, but he scourged Him anyway and "by His bruises we were healed."

Our Father, Hail Mary, Glory Be, Etc.
Additional clause: ...of thy womb, Jesus,
who patiently endured His suffering.

59

The Crowning with Thorns

"And platting a crown of thorns, they put it upon His head, and a reed in his hand."

Do good to thy friend before thou die, and according to thy ability, stretching out thy hand give to the poor.

- Matthew 27:29, Sirach 14:13

The crowning of thorns must have been a terrifying experience for Jesus. Not only did He endure the pain of the thorns pressed into His head but also the mockery and blows from these cruel strangers. They were like a pack of dogs ready to tear Him to shreds, "For many dogs have encompassed me: the council of the malignant hath besieged me."[43] To walk toward the throes of death is one thing but to go through it alone or in the company of strangers is another.

Many people will face death today in a similar fashion as Christ. They will be abandoned by friends and family and left with strangers who may not necessarily care. I must search for those people in the nursing homes, AIDS hospitals, and other places. I must go and comfort them in their dying hours and offer them the love of Christ. And for those who may be alone and dying, know that you are not alone. Jesus is always with you and has walked the path and bore the crown before you and for you.

Our Father, Hail Mary, Glory Be, Etc.
Additional clause: ...of thy womb, Jesus,
who is with me at the hour of death.

The Carrying of the Cross

And bearing his own cross, he went forth to that place which is called Calvary, but in Hebrew Golgotha.
Surely he hath borne our infirmities and carried our sorrows...

- John 19:17, Isaiah 53:4

"If any man will come after me, let him deny himself, and take up his cross daily, and follow me."[44] Guilt is one of the heaviest crosses associated with death. Guilt encourages me to imagine things would be different "if only". The cross of guilt can bring total destruction of one's life.

The biggest difference between Peter and Judas was that Peter allowed himself to be forgiven and forgave himself. This doesn't mean that those early morning hours spent in the courtyard by the fire didn't stay with Peter until his dying breath. But the forgiveness allowed him to go on instead of being disabled by his guilt.

Remorse, sorrow, and repentance are gifts from God. They can become my very own Simon of Cyrene helping me to carry my cross daily. They can strengthen me to do better and carry my cross farther. Surely many of the people who loved Jesus, especially His disciples, felt guilty for not doing more to help. They too suffered from the "if only" thoughts. However, when God's plan was fully revealed, they realized that God turns all things to good for those who love Him. In the midst of my guilt, I must not forget that God's plans for me are for good and not evil and in my weakness He makes me strong.

Our Father, Hail Mary, Glory Be, Etc.
Additional clause: ...of thy womb, Jesus,
who carried my guilt to Calvary

The Crucifixion and Death

And when they were come to the place which is called Calvary, they crucified him there...

And the Lord was pleased to bruise him in infirmity: if he shall lay down his life for sin, he shall see a long-lived seed, and the will of the Lord shall be prosperous in his hand. ...he hath borne the sins of many, and hath prayed for the transgressors.

- Luke 23:33, Isaiah 53:10,12

"Now there stood by the cross of Jesus, his Mother, and his mother's sister, Mary of Cleophas, and Mary Magdalen, When Jesus therefore had seen his mother and the disciple standing whom he loved..."[45] For a dying person to be surrounded by friends and family is a bittersweet gift from God. On one hand I would be comforted by having loved ones near. On the other hand I would hate to see the suffering my death is bringing to them.

The only dignified death is one that imitates Christ. It is a death that willingly embraces the cup of suffering without complaint. In order to help loved ones deal with my death I must comfort them in their time of loss. They are saddened because they will be losing me. Therefore, in the time that remains I must comfort them and give them all I have. I must remind them of the good times, give them what wisdom I have gained in this life, and assure them that I am at peace with them and God. Jesus was in tremendous agony from both the Crucifixion and seeing His loved ones suffering at the foot of the Cross. Yet He trusted in God's plan for Himself and them. I too must meet death with grace and strength. "Into thy hands I commend my spirit"[46]

Our Father, Hail Mary, Glory Be, Etc.
Additional clause: ...of thy womb, Jesus,
who is the comfort of the dying.

The Glorious Mysteries of Death
The Resurrection

And taking him down, he wrapped him in fine linen, and laid him in a sepulchre that was hewed in stone, wherein never yet any man had been laid.

I am a stranger and sojourner among you: give me the right of a burying place with you.

- Luke 23:53, Genesis 23:4

Cold stone welcomed the Savior. A cemetery can be a very cold place. One of the most chilling sites is the Arlington National Cemetery in Washington, D.C. Seemingly endless rows of white crosses mark the places of burial. The cold hard ground of a cemetery or sepulcher appears to welcome and swallow up the bodies of my loved ones. But as I walk through the cemetery paying respect and remembering my loved ones I must remember that they are merely sleeping. Eventually, on that great and terrible day, the graves will open and the rocks will cry out. Our bodies will be awakened from the sleep of death and be reunited with our souls. For Christ said, "I am the resurrection and the life: he that believeth in me, although he be dead, shall live."[47] On that day the cemeteries which are places now of mourning will be fields of rejoicing as the bodies and souls of the just are brought forth into the light of eternal day and they will hear Our Lord say, "Behold, I make all things new."[48] "Come my beloved enter into my rest."

Our Father, Hail Mary, Glory Be, Etc.
Additional clause: ...of thy womb, Jesus,
who rose from the dead.

The Ascension

This Jesus who is taken up from you into heaven, shall so come, as you have seen him going into heaven.

The chariot of God is attended by ten thousands; thousands of them that rejoice: the Lord is among them in Sina, in the holy place. Thou hast ascended on high, thou hast led captivity captive; thou hast received gifts in men.

- Acts of the Apostles 1:11, Psalm 67:18-19

All too often the last time I may see a deceased loved one is at the funeral home in his or her casket. I sometimes hate to even go and see them this way because this is not the memory of them I want burned into my mind. This still image is merely a shadow of the person I knew and loved. Jesus too was placed in a tomb and for many this was the last image they had of Him. However, He rose again and the last time many laid eyes on Him He was gloriously ascending into Heaven. Many of His followers stood on the Mount of Olives staring into the sky hoping to catch one more glimpse.

I must keep in mind the Ascension when I am faced with the loss of a loved one. I must remember that when I see them resting peacefully in the casket that they are merely sleeping and this is the last time I will see them in this world. Yet in the world to come I will see them as God sees them. When I stand watch in the funeral home, I must hear the voices of those angels saying to me, "Why are you looking down. This dear one who is taken from you will return to you more glorious than you can imagine."

Our Father, Hail Mary, Glory Be, Etc.
Additional clause: ...of thy womb, Jesus,
who will come again in glory.

The Descent of the Holy Spirit

*Because I have spoken these things to you, sorrow hath
filled your heart. But I tell you the truth; it is better for you that I
go; for if I go not the Paraclete will not come to you but if I go I
will send him to you.*

*the Lord gave, and the Lord hath taken away: as it hath
pleased the Lord, so is it done: blessed be the name of the Lord.*

- John 16:6-7, Job 1:21

As I write this meditation our community faces the loss of two
young men in their early twenties. Two thousand years removed it
is easy for me to see the necessity of Christ's death. However,
when death hits closer to home I have a hard time finding God's
reasons for the loss I suffer. I ask "Why"? I wonder what good
could possibly come from these seemingly pointless deaths.

No matter who is taken from me I must always search for God's
will and pray for the strength to accept it. As hard as death can be
to accept I must remember God has plans for me that are good and
never evil. Everything He does is designed to draw me closer to
Himself. Jesus had to leave so the Holy Spirit would come and
God could be closer to man, in fact, dwell within him. Maybe God
takes those who are dear to me so that they, like St. Therese of
Lisieux, may spend their heaven doing good on earth.

Our Father, Hail Mary, Glory Be, Etc.
Additional clause: ...of thy womb, Jesus,
who sends His Spirit in my time of need.

The Assumption of Mary

And there were given to the woman two wings of a great eagle that she might fly...unto her place.

He that feareth the Lord, honoureth his parents, and will serve them as his masters that brought him into the world.

- Revelation 12:14, Sirach 3:8

The loss of a parent can be crippling to a child no matter what the child's age. To watch an elderly parent slowly deteriorate in mind and body is a difficult thing. The once strong hands of a father now shake and tremble. The beautiful voice of a mother who long ago sang me to sleep now grows weak and tired. As the end of their journey here on earth draws closer I seem to cling even tighter to their words, their wisdom, and their very presence.

I can imagine too that the followers of Christ did not want Mary to be taken from them. They wanted to hear her song proclaiming the greatness of the Lord one more time. They needed her to stay and tell them stories about Jesus and the funny things He did growing up. The followers of Christ did not want to lose the woman they called Mother.

I need to make time for my parents while they are still with me. I should go for a walk with my father and take my mother to breakfast. I must try to learn from their lives and listen to every story they tell for they too will one day be taken from me. When my parents have passed on, I will remember them daily in my prayers. I will relive in my mind every good time and forget and forgive every bad time. I will entrust them to the Mother of God until we meet again in Heaven.

Our Father, Hail Mary, Glory Be, Etc.
Additional clause: ...of thy womb, Jesus,
who brought His Mother to Himself

The Coronation of Mary

*And a great sign appeared in heaven: A woman clothed
with the sun, and the moon under her feet, and on her head a
crown of twelve stars.*

*And the king said to me, and the queen that sat by him: For
how long shall thy journey be, and when wilt thou return? And it
pleased the king, and he sent me.*

- Nehemiah 2:6, Revelation 12:1

In the crowning of Mary I find the reward that awaits all those who
follow Christ. Mary shows me what awaits those followers of
Jesus who persevere to the end. Mary was not only the Mother of
Jesus but also the perfect follower of Him. She *is* the imitation of
Christ. To imitate Mary is to imitate Christ. After Mary's death
she was awakened by her Son and He brought her into the
heavenly kingdom. I must trust that after my death Jesus will
come to me also and lead me to the Heavenly Kingdom. There I
shall stand before the King of Kings and His Queen Mother for
eternity singing the praises of God and receiving a crown for
running the race to the end.

"Whoever seeks to save his life will lose it, but whoever loses his
life will save it." I must not fear death but seek to lose my life for
Christ so that I may inherit the Kingdom like Mary. I must seek to
spend my life for Christ so that I might, in the end, receive the
crown of victory.

Our Father, Hail Mary, Glory Be, Etc.
Additional clause: ...of thy womb, Jesus,
who sits with His Mother by His side.

The Mysteries of Addiction

"All the sins of your life seem to be rising up against you. Don't give up hope! On the contrary, call your holy mother Mary, with the faith and abandonment of a child. She will bring peace to your soul."

- St. Josemaria Escriva   *The Way # 498*

The Joyful Mysteries of Addiction

The Annunciation

Behold the handmaid of the Lord; be it done unto me according to thy word.

And the dragon was angry against the woman: and went to make war with the rest of her seed, who keep the commandments of God, and have the testimony of Jesus Christ.

- Luke 1:38, Revelation 12:17

I am afflicted by addiction, an addiction to sin. My addiction to sin is a negative mirror image of the Annunciation. I oftentimes say "yes" to things sinful and "no" to God, whereas Mary said "no" to everything sinful and "yes" to God.

Mary is often called the refuge of sinners. Might she also be called the refuge of the addicted? It does not matter what my addiction is, Mary can help. If I am addicted to drugs or alcohol, Mary can ask her Son to give me the wine that is His blood. If I am addicted to sexual sins, Mary can wrap me in her mantle of purity. If I am addicted to anger or power, Mary can obtain for me peace of heart and humility. Mary is my Mother who will never forsake me no matter how addicted I become. She will pull me out of the gutter when I am out of my mind with drugs. She will gently pull me away from the pornography and filth. She can talk me down from the precipice of anger and pride. In my darkest hour of addiction I must call on the Mother of God that she might obtain for me light from Light and release from the prison cell of addiction.

Our Father, Hail Mary, Glory Be, Etc.
Additional clause: ...of thy womb, Jesus,
who became like me in all things except sin.

69

The Visitation

And Mary rising up in those days, went into the hill country with haste into a city of Juda...And Mary abode with her about three months; and she returned to her own house.

My son, in thy sickness neglect not thyself, but pray to the Lord, and he shall heal thee.

- Luke 1:39, 56, Sirach 38:9

As one who is addicted I find there is comfort in Mary. Mary comes to visit me, like she did Elizabeth, without being asked. In fact she takes the initiative and goes "with haste" to help those in need. Once she entered into the home of Elizabeth and Zachary great things began to happen.

If I am drowning in my addiction Mary can help and she will come to me "with haste". Many times I am so unforgiving of myself and ashamed of my addiction. I feel there is no chance of forgiveness from Jesus. When I reach that point, the point where I am too ashamed to face the King of Kings, I must ask Mary into the house, as it were, of my heart. I must allow Mary to come into my life and help me get ready for Christ coming into my heart. Without even asking, if I am open, Mary will come and help me sweep out the addictions of my heart and prepare the way of the Lord. Let the Mother of Our Lord come to me as she did to Elizabeth and fill my heart with blessings and scatter the darkness of addiction.

Our Father, Hail Mary, Glory Be, Etc.
Additional clause: ...of thy womb, Jesus,
who can heal me through Mary.

The Nativity

...and they found Mary and Joseph, and the infant lying in the manger.

The Lord help him on his bed of sorrow: thou hast turned all his couch in his sickness. I said: O Lord, be thou merciful to me: heal my soul, for I have sinned against thee.

Luke 2:16, Psalm 40:4-5

How can this be - the King of Kings lying in a feeding trough for animals? It is absurd. How could this be - the Savior of mankind lying in such filth? To those without the eyes of faith it is simply another poor family down on their luck. In this present day I would be tempted to judge them. I might assume the father is just a lazy bum and the mother no good.

Too often I look at those who are addicted in the same way. Instead of seeing them as children of God, created in His image and likeness, I place my assumptions on them. Instead of reaching out to them in charity, I turn my head in disgust.

As an addict I know the shame that accompanies addiction. I know the fear of being looked down upon. I need help but am too proud to ask and those who have an idea about the truth of my addiction are too proud to offer their help. In the midst of my addiction I am like the infant in the manger. I am helpless and completely dependent on others to pick me up out of the filth. All I can do is cry out for help until someone shows me the way out of the darkness.

Please help those who are addicted. Look for Christ in the drunk, the prostitute, and the crack-addicted mother. But also look for Him in the mother and housewife who drinks heavily to deal with her children and family. Look for Him in the father who is spending his family's savings at the casino. Look for Him in the priest who struggles with the loneliness of his vocation. "Lord when did we see you..."

71

Our Father, Hail Mary, Glory Be, Etc.
Additional clause: ...of thy womb, Jesus,
who lifts me out of the filth of addiction.

The Presentation

And there was one Anna, ...who departed not from the temple, by fastings and prayers serving night and day.

Know ye that the Lord will hear your prayers, if you continue with perseverance in fastings and prayers in the sight of the Lord.

- Luke 2:36,37, Judith 4:11

In the Presentation I find great help for overcoming addiction. First I find the example of obedience in Mary and Joseph following the law of Moses. Even though they had had angels appear to them, shepherds and wise men seek them, and they knew the child was the Son of God, they fulfilled the precepts of the law.By following God's laws concerning the use of His gifts others, as well as I, will be blessed. When I am obedient to God's laws I am given the grace to overcome my addiction.

Secondly, I find Anna praying night and day. Only by constantly communicating with God can I know His will. Prayer enables my soul to respond generously to the Lord through selflessness. Prayer is essential to knowing God's will. When I follow God's will I will be released from my addiction.

Finally, I find an essential element to overcoming addiction - fasting. This does not merely mean to fast from that which I am addicted. I must also fast from that which is perfectly licit. Fasting strengthens the body and the will and gives mastery of self. In some cases only fasting can assist us in purging our addiction, "some demons can only be driven out by prayer and fasting."[49]

Our Father, Hail Mary, Glory Be, Etc.
Additional Clause...of they womb, Jesus,
who will purify me of my addiction

The Finding in the Temple

*And having fulfilled the days, when they returned, the child
Jesus remained in Jerusalem; and his parents knew it not. And
thinking that he was in the company, they came a day's journey,
and sought him among their kinsfolks and acquaintance. And not
finding him, they returned into Jerusalem, seeking him.*

*My son, in thy sickness neglect not thyself, but pray to the
Lord, and he shall heal thee.*

- Luke 2:43-45, Sirach 38:9

Each and every one of my actions affects those around me. No
man is an island and this is plainly seen in this last Joyful Mystery.
Jesus' staying behind in Jerusalem caused Mary and Joseph great
anguish and hardship. They were worried and I imagine His
extended family was concerned as well.

I am not alone in my addiction. My spouse, children, parents, and
Church are affected by my sins. My choice to delve deeper into
my addiction leaves my loved ones no choice but to be dragged
down with me. When they find me in the darkness of my addiction
I hear the words of Mary, "why have you treated us so?"

I must realize that sin is not only personal; it is communal and so is
addiction. The same addiction that makes my soul sick is the same
addiction that makes my marriage, family, and church sick. I must
learn to imitate Mary and seek Christ in my darkest hour and never
stop searching for Him. He will release the chains of my addiction
and then I will increase, "in wisdom and in stature, and in favor
with God and man."[50]

Our Father, Hail Mary, Glory Be, Etc.
Additional Clause…of thy womb, Jesus, in
whom I find help for my addictions.

The Luminous Mysteries of Addiction

The Baptism of Our Lord

And forthwith coming up out of the water, he saw the heavens opened, and the Spirit as a dove descending, and remaining on him. And there came a voice from heaven: Thou art my beloved Son; in thee I am well pleased.

And the serpent said to the woman: No, you shall not die the death. For God doth know that in what day soever you shall eat thereof, your eyes shall be opened: and you shall be as Gods, knowing good and evil.

- *Mark 1:10-11, Genesis 3:4-5*

When I think of mortal sins most often my mind turns toward sexual sins. In this present day that may be completely justified. Yet, too often I forget there is one sin that leads to all the others.[51] All of my addictions find their root and source of life in this sin. It is a sin that is completely undetectable without the aid of an abundance of God's grace. That sin is the sin of Pride. It is the sin of "me". It is in essence the "original sin". All of my addictions begin with pride. The sin of pride places me at the center of the universe and all things under my feet. I attempt to become like God, "Behold Adam is become as one of us, knowing good and evil."[52] Everything becomes a vehicle to self-satisfaction. Food, drink, money, sex, and power become a means to the end of self-love instead of selfless love.

This first Mystery of Light gives the cure or antidote for the sin of pride. It is humility. I can see tremendous displays of humility from John and Jesus. John's entire life has been given to the service of Christ and neighbor by preparing "the way of the Lord" in the hearts of the people. He knows his place for he says, "I must decrease so that he may increase, I am not fit to un-strap His sandal, It is you who should baptize me." Jesus shows me humility by being baptized, an act of repentance and conversion from sin.

75

At this moment in His life He symbolically drowns in the flood of our sins only to rise anew. As the new creation begins, as it did in the days of Noah, a dove appears above the waters. "Christ is baptized; let us also go down with Him, and rise with Him."[53] I must drown my addictions in the baptismal waters and arise a new, humble creation.

Our Father, Hail Mary, Glory Be, Etc.
Additional clause: ...of thy womb, Jesus,
who blessed the waters for baptism.

The Wedding at Cana

...the chief steward calleth the bridegroom, And saith to him: Every man at first setteth forth good wine, and when men have well drunk, then that which is worse. But thou hast kept the good wine until now.

Wine was created from the beginning to make men joyful, and not to make them drunk. Wine drunken with moderation is the joy of the soul and the heart. Sober drinking is health to soul and body. Wine drunken with excess raiseth quarrels; and wrath, and many ruins. Wine drunken with excess is bitterness of the soul.

- John 2:9c-10, Sirach 31:35-39

Everything in creation has its proper use and function. This includes alcohol and licit drugs. These can be used by man for joy and blessing if used properly: "wine to gladden men's hearts,"[54] and drugs to repair and heal the body.

The wedding at Cana shows that God intends for man to use His gifts for joy and happiness. Jesus turns water into wine thus blessing the wedding and probably keeping it from ruin. However, like all of God's gifts I have the ability to abuse them. When I become addicted to drugs and alcohol the blessings turn to curses. I find my "joy" not in the gift from the Giver but in the gift alone. In my addiction I stop praising the creator and start praising the creation.

All of my addictions are both spiritual and physical. They affect both my body and my soul. Therefore I must seek help on both levels. Jesus said that some demons can only be driven out through prayer and fasting. This is one of those demons. I must pray earnestly for help and not be afraid to ask others for their prayers as well. I must also place my body under my control and God's control through fasting. By fasting from not only the substances themselves but also from perfectly licit items I will again gain control over my body. I must also frequent the sacraments of reconciliation and the Eucharist. In penance I will find forgiveness, grace, and advice to conform myself more fully to Christ. In the Eucharist I will find, "the fruit of the vine and work of human hands that will become our spiritual drink. Blessed be God forever."

Our Father, Hail Mary, Glory Be, Etc.
Additional clause: ...of thy womb, Jesus,
who changed water into wine.

The Proclamation of the Kingdom

And seeing the multitudes, he went up into a mountain, and when he was set down, his disciples came unto him. And opening his mouth, he taught them...

All thy children shall be taught of [by] the Lord: and great shall be the peace of thy children.

- Matthew 5:1-2, Isaiah 54:13

The proclamation of the Kingdom begins with a litany of worldly contradictions on the mount. These contradictions are meant for today just as much as they were meant for the people on the hillside that day. For every blessing and promise of Jesus in the Beatitudes the world offers an addiction. The world always offers something good in the place of something better.

Jesus offers the promise of the everlasting Kingdom to those whose hearts are not set on riches. The world offers temporary but instant happiness to those who follow after wealth. Jesus promises the vision of God to those who are pure in heart. The world offers the power of God to those who have no concern for purity. As C.S. Lewis says through the words of the Senior Tempter Screwtape[55], "God cannot tempt to virtue as we [the devil and his angels] tempt to vice." There is a battle between two kingdoms taking place. The weapon of the kingdom of darkness is temptation that results in addiction to sin. The weapons of the Kingdom of God are the Beatitudes. Only by following these teachings of Christ can I overcome my addictions.

If I am poor and meek in spirit I can rely on the power of God to overcome my pride. By retaining my flavor and placing my light on a candlestick I can conquer the addiction to slothfulness. If I quell my anger and become merciful and even turn the other cheek I will be called a peacemaker. If I spiritually pluck out my eye or cut off my hand I will overcome my addiction to lust and so on. The antidotes to addiction are the Beatitudes.

Our Father, Hail Mary, Glory Be, Etc.
Additional clause: ...of thy womb, Jesus,
who has proclaimed the Kingdom in the Beatitudes

The Transfiguration

And it came to pass about eight days after these words, that he took Peter, and James, and John, and went up into a mountain to pray. And whilst he prayed, the shape of his countenance was altered, and his raiment became white and glittering. And behold two men were talking with him. And they were Moses and Elias, Appearing in majesty. And they spoke of his decease that he should accomplish in Jerusalem. But Peter and they that were with him were heavy with sleep. And waking, they saw his glory, and the two men that stood with him.

Thou who preparest the mountains by thy strength, being girded with power

- Luke 9:28-31, Psalm 64:7

The Luminous Mysteries are meant to shed light on the life of Christ and my own life. In these mysteries I find the light that shatters the darkness of addiction. A common yet often unseen addiction for most people is an addiction to power. One of my greatest fears is losing control of my perceived control. I am afraid to let go and let God. Untimely events and circumstances can appear to wreak havoc and spin my life out of control. I constantly feel the need to have control over my life and that often leads to wanting control over the lives of others. Eventually I find that I am controlled by this very desire for control.

God is in control of every aspect of my life. When I think I have control I am merely stepping in God's way and hindering His will. When Peter awoke from his nap he tried to gain control of the situation. He tried to do something that would put him back in control of what was happening in his life at that moment. I am quickly told that Peter "...knew not what he was saying." If I am to be clay in the potter's hands I must be soft, supple, and submissive. I cannot be hard and rigid trying to shape my own life. Even as Peter was speaking a cloud overshadowed them as if to remove the use of their senses so they could simply listen to the voice of God. "This is my beloved Son. He is in control and has all power. Listen to Him."

Our Father, Hail Mary, Glory Be, Etc.
Additional clause: ...of thy womb, Jesus,
who was transfigured on Mt. Tabor.

The Institution of the Eucharist

And whilst they were at supper, Jesus took bread, and blessed, and broke: and gave to his disciples, and said: Take ye, and eat. This is my body. And taking the chalice, he gave thanks, and gave to them, saying: Drink ye all of this. For this is my blood of the new testament, which shall be shed for many unto remission of sins.

Go not after thy lusts, but turn away from thy own will. If thou give to thy soul her desires, she will make thee a joy to thy enemies.

- Matthew26:26-28, Sirach 18:30-31

This mystery gives the antidote for perhaps the most prevalent addiction in the world today: sexual addiction. The Eucharist is the source and summit of the Christian life. I can find the light to disperse the darkness of every addiction in the Blessed Sacrament but most especially the darkness of sexual addiction. Jesus said, "this is my body which will be given up for you." I often say to myself and others, "this is my body." However I do not give it up for others; I keep it for myself. I essentially say, "this is my body which I will do with whatever I wish for my own pleasure."

Sexual addictions are some of the darkest addictions because they focus completely on self. In the midst of sexual addiction the devil places blinders on my eyes so that all that is visible is the sin before me. Like the garden long ago he presents it in such a way that I see the sin as, "good to eat, and fair to the eyes, and delightful to behold."[56] Immediately after a fall, as always, my persuasive tempter becomes a vicious, malignant accuser.

The Institution of the Eucharist is the antidote for sexual sins because it is the perfect example of the complete gift of self for others. My body is to be used as a vehicle to obtain grace for myself and others. Only by imitating Christ in giving my body, strength, and good works for the sake of others can I overcome the addiction to self abuse. If I can see Christ truly present in the

Eucharist I will be able to see Christ in others and in doing so overcome my addiction to pornography. Finally, by imitating Christ's gift of self to His bride on the cross I will be able to overcome my addiction to using my spouse for my own pleasure. Frequent reception of the Eucharist is the cure for the disease of sexual addiction. "Give us this day our daily bread. The bread that I give is my flesh for the life of the world."

Our Father, Hail Mary, Glory Be, Etc.
Additional clause: ...of thy womb, Jesus,
who gave me Himself in the Eucharist.

Sorrowful Mysteries of Addiction

The Agony in the Garden

And he was withdrawn away from them a stone's cast, and kneeling down, he prayed, Saying: Father, if thou wilt, remove this chalice from me: but yet not my will, but thine be done. And there appeared to him an angel from heaven, strengthening him. And being in an agony, he prayed the longer. And his sweat became as drops of blood, trickling down upon the ground.

Let nothing hinder thee from praying always, and be not afraid to be justified even to death: for the reward of God continueth for ever.

- Luke 22:41-44, Sirach 18:22

Addictions can cause some of the most painful agony known to man. The agony comes when I have full knowledge of my sinfulness yet feel paralyzed to overcome it. I fear the slightest temptation yet I will not resist to the point of shedding blood.

Christ experienced and took on the agony of my addictions. In the darkness on the Mount of Olives He fell to His knees in prayer as the temptations of my addictions approached. He fought my addictions not with legions of angels or bands of apostles but alone in prayer. Christ has overcome the world and He has overcome my addictions. I now have three choices before me in my own "Agony in the Garden" as it were when faced with a temptation towards my addiction. First, I can imitate Christ and recommit myself more earnestly to prayer even to the point of shedding blood.[57] Second, I can imitate the apostles and close my eyes to the situation and fall asleep spiritually hoping that when I awake it will be a new day. However, I know this will not happen. The apostles were awakened by a blood-and-sweat-soaked Jesus rebuking them for not praying with Him for just one hour. Lastly, I can choose to imitate Judas and betray the Lord with a kiss. I can give Him "lip service" yet keep my heart far from conversion and union with His agony.

Lord, help me to trust in You and pray and choose "death rather than sin," death rather than my addiction. "Dost thou betray the Son of Man with a kiss?"[58]

Our Father, Hail Mary, Glory Be, Etc.
Additional clause: ...of thy womb, Jesus,
who suffered in the Garden for my addictions.

The Scourging at the Pillar

Then therefore, Pilate took Jesus, and scourged him.
Surely he hath borne our infirmities and carried our
sorrows: and we have thought him as it were a leper, and as one
struck by God and afflicted. But he was wounded for our
iniquities, he was bruised for our sins: the chastisement of our
peace was upon him, and by his bruises we are healed. All we like
sheep have gone astray, every one hath turned aside into his own
way: and the Lord hath laid on him the iniquity of us all.

- John 19:1, Isaiah 53:4-6

At the scourging at the pillar Jesus took upon Himself the intense physical sufferings of my addictions. His flesh was torn open with each lash of the whip by my addiction to sins of the flesh. His wounds poured forth the dark red blood for my addiction to alcohol and drugs. He was stripped for the scourging for my addiction to pride. He was strapped and secured to the pillar for my addiction to power. Yet, as Isaiah says, "by his bruises, we are healed."

Jesus has taken the physical punishment for my addictions. I must keep the image of Christ being scourged ever fresh in my mind. If I am resisting and overcoming my addiction I will see the scourged body of Jesus as a beautiful gift to me. If I am not resisting with all of my strength I will see His scourging as meaningless and will one day discover the whip in my own hand. However, Jesus will be, "dumb as a lamb before his shearer and he shall not open his mouth."[59]

Our Father, Hail Mary, Glory Be, Etc.
Additional clause: ...of thy womb, Jesus,
who was scourged for my addictions.

87

The Crowning with Thorns

And platting a crown of thorns, they put it upon his head,
and a reed in his right hand. And bowing the knee before him, they
mocked him, saying: Hail, king of the Jews. And spitting upon him,
they took the reed, and struck his head.

For day and night thy hand was heavy upon me: I am
turned in my anguish, whilst the thorn is fastened.

I have given my body to the strikers, and my cheeks to them
that plucked them: I have not turned away my face from them that
rebuked me, and spit upon me.

- Mark 17:19, Psalm 31:4, Isaiah 50:6

The second gate which guards against addiction, after the eye, is the mind. Through the mind thoughts race of how to use or abuse God's gifts. The mind, when guided by an upright heart, will stand fast against temptation and addiction. The mind alone, without the heart, will excuse and reason away God's laws.

God knows what I need before I ask and knows all of my thoughts. Jesus suffered the cruel crowning of thorns for my sinfulness of thought. Every thorn and blow to the head brought Him intense suffering. He experienced the suffering that accompanies the mental battles of addiction.

I have a crown of victory waiting for me if I only endure the crown of thorns in this life. This crown of thorns comes from blocking all sinful thoughts, images, and desires from taking over my mind. It is no easy crown to wear or endure but it is mine alone. I must set my face against the blows of the enemy and all his temptations.

Lord, help me to echo the words of the prophet Isaiah when I am faced with temptations toward my addiction. "The Lord God is my helper, therefore I am not confounded: therefore I have set my face as a most hard rock: and I know that I shall not be confounded."[60]

Our Father, Hail Mary, Glory Be, Etc.

Additional clause: ...of thy womb, Jesus,
who bore the crown for my addictions.

The Carrying of the Cross

And the whole people answering, said: His blood be upon us and our children

And bearing his own cross, he went forth to that place which is called Calvary, but in Hebrew Golgotha.

Why then is thy apparel red, and thy garments like theirs that tread in the winepress? I have trodden the winepress alone, and of the Gentiles there is not a man with me: I have trampled on them in my indignation, and have trodden them down in my wrath, and their blood is sprinkled upon my garments, and I have stained all my apparel. I looked about, and there was none to help: I sought, and there was none to give aid: and my own arm hath saved for me, and my indignation itself hath helped me.

- Matt 27:25, John 19:17, Isaiah 63:2-3,5

The wood of the cross most likely weighed as much as Jesus did Himself. He was forced to carry this cross even after the cruel torture He had previously endured. However, the weight of Christ's cross was not a weight of oak or cedar or any other wood. The weight of His cross was the weight of my addictions. He carried the weight of the extra food from my gluttony. His cross clanked and jingled under the weight of empty whiskey bottles and crack pipes. The impure images from adult magazines flapped in the wind on the path to Calvary. Christ carried them all on His shoulder. The weight was tremendous and caused Him to fall. Yet as an example He stood once more and continued on, determined to crucify my addictions on that hill outside Jerusalem. "The Lord laid on him the iniquity of us all."[61]

He did not lay down that cross nor can I. I must carry my cross daily and bring my addictions to Calvary to be crucified. When I fall I cannot stay down or the weight of the cross will crush me. I must rise and continue my journey. When Jesus says, "follow me", He means to Calvary.

Our Father, Hail Mary, Glory Be, Etc.

Additional clause: ...of thy womb, Jesus,
who carried the cross of my addictions

The Crucifixion and Death

And it was the third hour, and they crucified him.
For many dogs have encompassed me: the council of the malignant hath besieged me. They have dug my hands and feet.
And they shall say to him: What are these wounds in the midst of thy hands? And he shall say: With these I was wounded in the house of them that loved me.

- Mark 15:25, Psalm 21:17, Zechariah 13:6

On the cross Lord Jesus You took upon Yourself all of my addictions. You, who were without sin, became sin that I might have eternal life. You, purity Incarnate, were stripped naked in the midst of all for my sexual addictions. Your only possession, Your seamless garment, was taken from You for my addiction to things, and the soldiers gambled to win it. You took my addiction to anger and violence and allowed Your hands and feet to be pierced. You Jesus, meek and humble of heart, were lifted up for all to see and ridicule for my addiction to pride. You, who were called a drunk and a glutton, drank the sour wine for my addictions to food and alcohol. You took the punishment and death my addictions deserve and nailed them to the cross. When You had done all of this You said, "It is finished."[62] Sin and addiction were finished. Their power was put to death on the cross.

Lord, help me to trust in this one saving act and constantly participate in it by bringing my sin and addiction to Mass and washing myself clean in Your blood. "These are they who are come out of great tribulation, and have washed their robes, and have made them white in the blood of the Lamb."[63]

Our Father, Hail Mary, Glory Be, Etc.
Additional clause: ...of thy womb, Jesus,
who put my addictions to death on the cross.

The Glorious Mysteries of Addiction

The Resurrection

When she had thus said, she turned herself back, and saw Jesus standing; and she knew not that it was Jesus. Jesus saith to her: Woman, why weepest thou? whom seekest thou? She, thinking it was the gardener, saith to him: Sir, if thou hast taken him hence, tell me where thou hast laid him, and I will take him away. Mary Magdalen cometh, and telleth the disciples: I have seen the Lord, and these things he said to me.

Now God hath both raised up the Lord, and will raise us up also by his power.

- John 20:14-15,18, 1 Corinthians 6:14

It is said that the only things in heaven that are manmade are the wounds of Christ. In His resurrected body He retained the wounds of crucifixion.

My addictions can wear my body out and even cause physical and spiritual scarring. Christ has overcome the world, sin, and death. He has overcome my addictions. If I have followed Him to death on Calvary I can follow Him to life eternal. My body too will be renewed and made glorious in the resurrection at the end of time. Until then I am to treat my body as a temple of the Holy Spirit. I must prepare myself for this eternal life by treating my body with honor and respect. I must put away the addictions that cause damage to my body as well as to my soul. When I, like St. Paul, put on Christ and no longer live but have Christ living in me, others, like Mary Magdalene, will not recognize me. When I finally reveal myself to them and they see that I have changed and put away my old self and have become a "new man" they again, like Mary, will run and tell the world they have seen the power of the risen Lord.

Our Father, Hail Mary, Glory Be, Etc.

93

Additional clause: ...of thy womb, Jesus,
who will raise me up on the last day free from addiction.

The Ascension

*And when he had said these things, while they looked on,
he was raised up: and a cloud received him out of their sight.*

*The night is passed, and the day is at hand. Let us therefore
cast off the works of darkness, and put on the armour of light. Let
us walk honestly, as in the day: not in rioting and drunkenness, not
in chambering and impurities, not in contention and envy: But put
ye on the Lord Jesus Christ, and make not provision for the flesh in
its concupiscences.*

- Acts of the Apostles 1:9, Romans 13:12-14

One of the greatest fears of any addict is that he will be caught.
Yet at the same time his desire is to be discovered so he may begin
healing.

A desire to be found out always echoes somewhere in the darkness
of my mind. It is certainly a self-conscious cry for help. The
angels on the Mount of Olives tell me that Jesus will return in
much the same way as He left. However, Jesus said that I will not
know the day nor the hour of His return. He will return like a thief
in the night.

This mystery of the Ascension reminds me that Jesus is coming
back. It also compels me to re-examine my life and ponder what I
might be doing when He does return. Will I be squandering my
family's savings at the blackjack table or lottery machine? Will I
be hiding in the garage or bathroom drinking booze? Will I be
raising my fist and voice to those people I am commissioned to
love? Will I be surfing adult websites or looking through explicit
magazines when the Lord appears in all His glory? To be caught
in my addiction by a friend, family member, or co-worker is one
thing. To be caught by Christ at His second-coming is another.

Our Father, Hail Mary, Glory Be, Etc.
Additional clause: ...of thy womb, Jesus,
who will return when I least expect Him.

The Descent of the Holy Spirit

And when they were come in, they went up into an upper room... All these were persevering with one mind in prayer with the women, and Mary the mother of Jesus, and with his brethren.

He that is a friend loveth at all times: and a brother is proved in distress.

A faithful friend is a strong defense: and he that hath found him, hath found a treasure.

- Acts of the Apostles 1:13-14, Proverbs 17:17, Sirach 6:14

In this mystery God gives me an excellent help in overcoming my addictions. No man is an island, yet as an addict I often feel as though I am the only person on the face of the earth. The addiction makes me focus so completely on myself that everyone else fades from the picture. When my addiction is exposed, again I am alone and become an outcast of my friends, family, and society.

In this mystery I am shown that the Body of Christ is a community of believers. This community is one of God's greatest gifts to an addict. By belonging to a group of believers I am able to graft myself into the Body of Christ and receive innumerable graces, the foremost being the Holy Spirit Himself. I also gain the prayers and sacrifices of others made on my behalf. This group of believers will also hold me accountable for my actions. They will pray for me, admonish me to do better, and pick me up when I fall. To truly conquer my addictions I must surround myself with believing people who will commit themselves to prayer and who will influence me in positive ways and hold me accountable. *Come Holy Spirit, fill the hearts of your faithful and enkindle in them the fire of your love. Send forth your Spirit and they shall be created. And you shall renew the face of the earth.*

Our Father, Hail Mary, Glory Be, Etc.
Additional clause: ...of thy womb, Jesus,
who sends the Holy Spirit to help me overcome my addiction.

The Assumption of Mary

And the king shall greatly desire thy beauty; for he is the Lord thy God, and him they shall adore.

...the body is not for fornication, but for the Lord, and the Lord for the body. Now God hath both raised up the Lord, and will raise us up also by his power.

- Psalm 44:12, 1 Corinthians 6:13b-14

Jesus loved His mother too much to allow her body to see corruption in the grave so He brought her to Himself. Mary's focus in life was God and doing His will namely by loving her Son. Like Mary, the closer I come to Christ the closer He comes to me. When He is lifted up as the center of my life He will draw me to Himself. All addictions lead me further away from Christ. With the help of Mary, the grace of God, and a firm resolution to turn more fully to Jesus I can overcome my addictions. When I turn away from sin and place it behind me I begin my journey back home to my Father's house. The closer I get to Him the closer He will get to me until eventually He begins running to meet me.

Lord, I resolve to imitate Mary more fully and place Christ in the center of my life and look with joyful hope for the day when He will call me to Himself. "From them that resist thy right hand keep me, as the apple of thy eye. Protect me under the shadow of thy wings."[64]

Our Father, Hail Mary, Glory Be, Etc.
Additional clause: ...of thy womb, Jesus,
who draws me out of addiction to Himself.

97

The Coronation of Mary

For know you this and understand, that no fornicator, or unclean, or covetous person (which is a serving of idols), hath inheritance in the kingdom of Christ and of God.

I am the mother of fair love, and of fear, and of knowledge, and of holy hope. In me is all grace of the way and of the truth, in me is all hope of life and of virtue.

- Ephesians 5:5, Sirach 24:24-25

Scripture tells me that nothing unclean can enter heaven. I cannot enter into the Kingdom and still cling to my addictions. As Our Lord said, "You cannot serve God and Mammon."[65] Mary served God wholeheartedly on earth and continues to do so in heaven. She who is my Mother[66] is also my Queen. The Queen of Heaven and earth can obtain for me from her Son, the King, all graces necessary for overcoming my addictions. God has seen fit to distribute His grace through the intercession of His Mother so I must acknowledge her title of Mediatrix of all Graces. And so scripture says of her, "I, like a brook out of a river of a mighty water; I, like a channel of a river, and like an aqueduct, came out of paradise. I said: I will water my garden of plants, and I will water abundantly the fruits of my meadow"[67]. Therefore, I trust in so wonderful an intercessor and trust in her unceasing prayers for me. She will obtain all the graces I need to overcome my addictions and in doing so place me in the service of her Son the King of Kings.

Our Father, Hail Mary, Glory Be, Etc.
Additional clause: ...of thy womb, Jesus,
who gave me His mother as Queen.

The Mysteries of Marriage

"The way of love has a name: it is *Sacrifice*."

- St. Josemaria Escriva   *The Forge # 768*

The Joyful Mysteries of Marriage

The Annunciation
And the angel answering, said to her: The Holy Ghost shall come upon thee, and the power of the most High shall overshadow thee. And therefore also the Holy which shall be born of thee shall be called the Son of God. And Mary said: Behold the handmaid of the Lord; be it done to me according to thy word. And the angel departed from her.

Suffer the little children to come unto me, and forbid them not; for of such is the kingdom of God.

- Luke 1:35,38, Mark 10:14

"Be it done unto me according to thy word." With these words heaven was married to earth. Mary said, "I do", and conceived a Son by her spouse, the Holy Spirit, and the world has never been the same. Love manifests itself within marriage in the bringing forth of offspring. For those who cannot conceive children physically they are to manifest their love through spiritual offspring. When a couple is married, the Church asks them to promise to accept children lovingly from God and raise them according to the teachings of the Church. To which they agree without much thought yet a large majority of professed Catholic married couples employ the use of artificial contraception. Has that promise made on our wedding day turned into a lie and denial of God's will? Every human life brought forth changes the course of human history. If we keep our promise to God and His Church it changes history for the good and furthers the Kingdom of God. If we do not keep our promise we are living a lie and helping bring about the destruction of the Kingdom. Contraception has no place in our marriage. We promise to accept children lovingly from God. Be it done unto us according to thy word.

Our Father, Hail Mary, Glory Be, Etc.
Additional clause: ...of thy womb, Jesus,

who gives life to our marriage.

The Visitation

And Mary rising up in those days, went into the hill country with haste into a city of Juda. And she entered into the house of Zachary, and saluted Elizabeth. And it came to pass, that when Elizabeth heard the salutation of Mary, the infant leaped in her womb. And Elizabeth was filled with the Holy Ghost: And she cried out with a loud voice, and said: Blessed art thou among women, and blessed is the fruit of thy womb.

A good wife is a good portion, she shall be given in the portion of them that fear God, to a man for his good deeds. Rich or poor, if his heart is good, his countenance shall be cheerful at all times.

- Luke 1:39-42, Sirach 26:3-4

We often see evangelization as something we do to our friends and neighbors but not our spouse. To truly love, honor, and obey we must bring Christ, like Mary, to our spouse. We must also, like Elizabeth, see Christ in our spouse.

The Visitation gives a perfect example of how we should treat our husband or wife. First, we must always go "with haste" to meet their needs even before we are asked. Jesus came to serve and not to be served and we should adopt this attitude. Second, we should recognize Christ in our spouse. We should focus, no matter how difficult, on the fact that they too are created in the image and likeness of God. If we treat them with this type of respect we will help them realize their value and worth as children of God. Finally, we should rejoice in our spouse and magnify God for the wonderful gift that they are. We can rejoice in them by setting aside time to spend together on the couch, talking, walking or studying scripture. We can magnify the Lord by bringing Christ to them in prayer, example, and spiritual growth. "In like manner also let wives be subject to their husbands: that if any believe not the word, they may be won without the word, by the conversation of the wives…Ye husbands, likewise dwelling with them according to knowledge, giving honour to the female as to the weaker vessel, and as to the co-heirs of the grace of life: that your prayers be not hindered."[68]

Our Father, Hail Mary, Glory Be, Etc.
Additional clause: ...of thy womb, Jesus,
who will bring conversion into our marriage.

The Nativity

And Joseph rising up from sleep, did as the angel of the Lord had commanded him, and took unto him his wife.

And she brought forth her firstborn son, and wrapped him up in swaddling clothes, and laid him in a manger; because there was no room for them in the inn.

- Matt 1:24, Luke 2:7

Mary was due to deliver her child at any time and either had to walk or ride a donkey. Joseph hadn't slept much lately and had been walking for miles only to find there was no room at the inn. Life has many unexpected and unforeseen experiences waiting around each and every corner. Strength and resolve is needed to keep a marriage together during these times of trial. Unexpected expenses, illness, loss of job or possessions, and special-needs children can stress and strain a marriage to the breaking point.

When we feel those pressures we must turn wholeheartedly to the example of the Holy Family. Even during the most trying times they followed God's will and were blessed richly for doing so. Joseph could have left Mary and the child that wasn't his but instead he chose to adopt. Mary could have gone back to Elizabeth's to give birth to her Son but she chose to stay by her husband's side. Joseph could have left Mary when he discovered Herod was coming for the child but he stayed and loved and protected them both. The Holy Family shows us that married life is not always easy but it is well worth the effort. What God has joined together let us not put asunder by our selfishness but instead let us adopt the selflessness of Mary and Joseph even in the most difficult situations.

Our Father, Hail Mary, Glory Be, Etc.
Additional clause: ...of thy womb, Jesus,
who is with us in the trying times of marriage.

The Presentation

*And after the days of her purification, according to the law
of Moses, were accomplished, they carried him to Jerusalem, to
present him to the Lord: As it is written in the law of the Lord:
Every male opening the womb shall be called holy to the Lord:
And to offer a sacrifice, according as it is written in the law of the
Lord, a pair of turtledoves, or two young pigeons:*

*And if her hand find not sufficiency, and she is not able to
offer a lamb, she shall take two turtles [turtledoves], or two young
pigeons, one for a holocaust, and another for sin: and the priest
shall pray for her, and so she shall be cleansed.*

- Luke 2:22-24, Leviticus 12:8

The Presentation shows us the result of faithfulness to the laws of
God by married people. Did the Mother of God and her husband
need to fulfill the law? After all it does seem a bit redundant;
offering God to God.

For a married couple trying to follow the laws of God many things
can appear to be pointless or redundant. However, we must see
that God has blessings in store for us and others that can only come
through our faithfulness to His commandments. Our daily
observance of His commands will bring "light for revelation" to
those around us. By following the example of Mary and Joseph
and bringing all we have and placing it before God we show the
world that our "eyes have seen the salvation" prepared for the
world. Our faithfulness to God and each other shows those around
us that God's design is for us to become "one flesh". The law of
Moses calls for a lamb, a young pigeon, or a turtle dove. It also
states that if the woman cannot afford a lamb she may bring two
turtle doves or two pigeons. Mary and Joseph fulfilled the law to
the greatest of their ability, as should we. They not only brought
the two birds they also brought the Lamb.

Lord, help us to offer to you our marriage. Help us to be faithful to your commands and to each other and in doing so lead others closer to you.

Our Father, Hail Mary, Glory Be, Etc.
Additional clause: ...of thy womb, Jesus,
who has purified our marriage with His blood.

The Finding in the Temple

And seeing him, they wondered. And his mother said to him: Son, why hast thou done so to us? behold thy father and I have sought thee sorrowing. And he said to them: How is it that you sought me? did you not know, that I must be about my father's business? And they understood not the word that he spoke unto them. And he went down with them, and came to Nazareth, and was subject to them. And his mother kept all these words in her heart.

Blessed are all they that fear the Lord: that walk in his ways. Thy wife as a fruitful vine, on the sides of thy house. Thy children as olive plants, round about thy table.

- Luke 2:48-51, Psalm 127:1,3

The finding in the Temple is a culminating lesson on the need for strong, faithful, loving husbands to make marriage work. Joseph suffered so much physically in protecting and providing for Mary and her Son. Here at the Temple, he suffers emotionally. The boy, who he knows is not his own, asks a question that pierces Joseph's heart, "Did you not know, that I must be about my Father's business?"

Many of today's men are spiritually weak. Joseph's example says to us married men, "fear not, only believe".[69] Joseph shows how to deal with every situation in marriage from infidelity to children to work. Joseph never says one word but like a perfect follower of Christ, his example says more than a few verses could ever say. Joseph endured all things, sacrificed all self-desires, and placed himself at the service of Mary and Jesus. If we husbands will follow his example, our wives will take and keep these things in their hearts and our children will become lovingly obedient to us.

Our Father, Hail Mary, Glory Be, Etc.
Additional clause: ...of thy womb, Jesus,
who strengthens husbands who are faithful.

The Luminous Mysteries of Marriage

The Baptism of Jesus

And I knew him not; but he who sent me to baptize with water, said to me: He upon whom thou shalt see the Spirit descending, and remaining upon him, he it is that baptizeth with the Holy Ghost. And I saw, and I gave testimony, that this is the Son of God.

Jesus answered: Amen, amen I say to thee, unless a man be born again of water and the Holy Ghost, he cannot enter into the kingdom of God.

- John 2:33-34, 3:5

A wedding ring is a symbol of the love between husband and wife. It is also a symbol of the love of God. This love, like the ring, has no end. It is also a symbol of a new creation. When the husband and wife wear their wedding rings they give witness to the world that they are a new creation. The two have become one and one ring cannot be seen without giving thought to the other.

An act that is almost completely hidden and unseen in the wedding ceremony is the blessing of the rings. The priest blesses the rings with water thereby blessing them and the sacrament which they represent. The rings also symbolize death and rebirth; the death of two individuals and the rebirth of one creature ordained by God to "be fruitful and multiply".

Without Christ and the Holy Spirit the marriage ceremony is merely symbolic like the baptism of John with no effectual grace. However, when Christ and the Holy Spirit are present in the marriage ceremony, we see Christ in the new creation of "one flesh" and the Holy Spirit descending and blessing the man and woman. Let us be mindful of not only our baptismal vows each time we bless ourselves with Holy Water but let us also be mindful of our wedding vows.

Our Father, Hail Mary, Glory Be, Etc.
Additional clause: ...of thy womb, Jesus,
who was baptized by John.

The Wedding at Cana

And the third day, there was a marriage in Cana of
Galilee: and the mother of Jesus was there.

And the Lord God said: It is not good for man to be alone:
let us make him a helper like unto himself. Wherefore a man shall
leave father and mother, and shall cleave to his wife: and they
shall be two in one flesh.

- John 2:1, Genesis 2:18,24

Here, in John's Gospel, we find Jesus at a wedding in Cana. Our
meditation could simply end here by saying that Jesus needs to be
present in our marriage in order for it to be fruitful. However, God
calls us much deeper into the beauty of marriage in this mystery.

The Gospel of John in many ways is a parallel to Genesis and other
Old Testament books. Both Genesis and John begin in the same
manner reminding us that God created everything including
marriage. Marriage has been a sacred event ordained by God since
the beginning. God sanctified marriage by being a witness of the
first wedding and now begins His earthly ministry at this marriage
in Cana. The mystery of marriage is as deep as the mystery of
God's power. God commands husband and wife to be fruitful and
multiply. To be married is sacred because it is to share on this
earth a power with God to create. Husband and wife are given a
power no other creature possesses. They have the power to co-
create an immortal being. With the help of God married men and
women create beings made in the image and likeness of God.
They help create beings that find they had a beginning but their
existence will have no end. Only God can create but he allows us
to help. He allows us to fill the jars.

Our Father, Hail Mary, Glory Be, Etc.
Additional clause: ...of thy womb, Jesus,
who changed water into wine.

The Proclamation of the Kingdom

Jesus came into Galilee, preaching the gospel of the kingdom of God, And saying: The time is accomplished, and the kingdom of God is at hand: repent, and believe the gospel.

For our wrestling is not against flesh and blood; but against principalities and power, against the rulers of the world of this darkness, against the spirits of wickedness in the high places. Therefore take unto you the armour of God, that you may be able to resist in the evil day, and to stand in all things perfect

- Mark 1:14-15, Ephesians 6:12-13

When Jesus started His ministry He began with these words, "Do penance, for the kingdom of God is at hand."[70] The Kingdom of God is here now. It is at hand right in front of us. Christ opened the gates and every moment battles are taking place to further advance the front line and expand the Kingdom.

Even though we may be at a distant outpost on the forefront of newly taken territory we are still in the Kingdom. How far the Kingdom advances depends a great deal on how we live our lives especially in the context of our marriage. We can apply all of the *Beatitudes* to our married life but none more readily than the teaching on adultery. Adultery does not necessarily need to be physical. As Jesus teaches, even lusting is adultery. In fact, this is how infidelity most often starts, through the eye and into the mind affecting the body. That is why Christ follows this teaching directly with teachings on removing the eye or any other body part that may lead us into scandal.

We, as a married couple, can be a powerful force in the battle for the Kingdom. Is it any wonder that Satan would attack marriage so vigorously? Prayerful married people not only fight tremendous battles for the Kingdom but also support and carry each other when wounded. Married couples are also the source and trainers of future warriors. For this reason Satan tries to lay waste to families. The Kingdom of God is at hand. Repent, be healed, and do battle.

111

Our Father, Hail Mary, Glory Be, Etc.
Additional clause: ...of thy womb, Jesus,
who calls us to do battle for the Kingdom.

The Transfiguration

*And after six days Jesus taketh unto him Peter and James,
and John his brother, and bringeth them up into a high mountain
apart: And he was transfigured before them. And his face did
shine as the sun: and his garments became white as snow. And
behold there appeared to them Moses and Elias talking with him.
And Peter answering, said to Jesus: Lord, it is good for us to be
here: if thou wilt, let us make here three tabernacles, one for thee,
and one for Moses, and one for Elias.*

*And the Lord said to Moses: Come up to me into the mount,
and be there; and I will give thee tables of stone, and the law. And
the sight of the glory of the Lord, was like a burning fire upon the
top of the mount, in the eyes of the children of Israel.*

- Matthew 17:1-4, Exodus 24:12a, 17

Peter, James, and John followed reluctantly. Their legs began to
ache at the sight of the mountain. They may have been thinking of
ways to stop or divert Jesus. From a distance the mountain
appeared insurmountable. As they approached the mountain it
appeared to grow larger and as they began their assent the air grew
thinner, their bodies seemed to become heavier, and their legs
weaker.

Married couples can easily associate with the feelings of these
three men following Christ. Problems that arise in marriage can
appear insurmountable only to become even more difficult when
the problem is in their midst. These mountains can include
children, finances, infidelity, change of jobs, death in the family,
and many, many more. The only way a married couple can climb
and conquer these mountains is by staying together and by
following Jesus. If we continue our journey, no matter how
difficult, we will arrive at the top, look at where we have been and
say, like Peter, "it is good for us to be here". We may also find
that our spouse and in fact our marriage has been transfigured by
the experience and is glowing with the radiance of God.

113

Our Father, Hail Mary, Glory Be, Etc.
Additional clause: ...of thy womb, Jesus,
who asks us to follow Him up the mountain.

The Institution of the Eucharist

the bread that I will give, is my flesh, for the life of the world

> *Husbands, love your wives, as Christ also loved the church, and delivered himself up for it: That he might sanctify it, cleansing it by the laver of water in the word of life: That he might present it to himself a glorious church, not having spot or wrinkle, or any; such thing; but that it should be holy, and without blemish.*

- John 6:52b, Ephesians 5:25-27

During the Last Supper we find Christ offering Himself to His followers. Christ gives Himself freely saying, "this is my body". It is truly His flesh. It is the entire sacrifice of Christ in an unbloody manner like the sacrifice of the Mass. Through study of the Scriptures and the understanding of the early Church Fathers, we understand that the Last Supper, the sacrifice on Calvary, and the wedding feast of the Lamb mentioned in the book of Revelation are all one in the same. Like the Trinity, three distinct and equal parts yet all of them the exact same event, the exact same sacrifice.

The renewal of the marriage covenant at the marriage bed is a parallel to this event. Christ gave His flesh to His bride the Church, and continues to do so for the life of the world. Likewise, the husband gives his flesh to his bride, his wife, and continues to do so for the life of the marriage and the family. Like the Church, the wife, receives her husband and gives new life to her family.

Jesus gave himself completely without reserve or selfishness and the Church receives him willingly, lovingly, and brings forth new life abundantly. Our marriage should imitate this heavenly marriage. Total self-giving and openness to life are the marks of a sanctifying marriage.

Our Father, Hail Mary, Glory Be, Etc.
Additional clause: ...of thy womb, Jesus,

who gives us His flesh in the Eucharist.

The Sorrowful Mysteries of Marriage

The Agony in the Garden

And he was withdrawn away from them a stone's cast; and kneeling down, he prayed, Saying: Father, if thou wilt, remove this chalice from me: but yet not my will, but thine be done. And there appeared to him an angel from heaven, strengthening him. And being in an agony, he prayed the longer. And his sweat became as drops of blood, trickling down upon the ground.

Submit thyself then to him, and be at peace: and thereby thou shalt have the best fruits.

- Luke 22:41-44, Job 22:21

So many things can cause agony within marriage. We can be in agony with our spouse or because of our spouse. Differing views on finance, children, and the future can cause agonizing times of cold silence or heated arguments. Different faith backgrounds and different views on sex within the context of marriage can be the cause of tremendous stress and agony. The loss of a job or legal problems can cause agony in marriage seemingly to the point of sweating blood.

When we say, "I do", to each other we say, "your will, not mine", to God. If we are accepting of our cup of sufferings within marriage God will send His angel to minister to us. This angel may be in the form of a counselor, new job, sound advice from a friend, or just an ear that will listen. Nevertheless, God asks us to accept His will for our marriage. When we are in agony within our marriage let us heed the words of Christ and in doing so be strengthened to accept the cup, "Watch ye, and pray that ye enter not into temptation. The spirit indeed is willing, but the flesh weak. "71

Our Father, Hail Mary, Glory Be, Etc.
Additional clause: ...of thy womb, Jesus,

117

who was in agony for our marriage.

The Scourging at the Pillar

I am innocent of the blood of this just man; look you to it.
And the whole people answering, said: His blood be upon us and
our children. Then he released to them Barabbas, and having
scourged Jesus, delivered him unto them to be crucified.

So also ought men to love their wives as their own bodies.
He that loveth his wife, loveth himself. For no man ever hated his
own flesh; but nourisheth and cherisheth it, as also Christ doth the
church.

- Matt 27:24-26, Ephesians 5:28-29

Jesus suffered the scourging at the pillar for abuse within marriage.
Many marriages today are stricken with abuse. It can be subtle and
sometimes unseen even by those who are being abused. It can also
be obvious and brutal, visibly noticed by the outside world. Many
men and women suffer from emotional abuse from a spouse who
toys with feelings and emotions as a form of control. Others suffer
spiritual abuse when a spouse ridicules and belittles them because
of their faith. Some spouses suffer from sexual abuse ranging from
immoral sex acts to rape. Many men and women suffer from
terrible physical abuse at the hands of their spouse.

Jesus took these abuses upon Himself at the scourging. He also
gave us a courageous example by quietly enduring His suffering
and praying for His abusers. Anyone in an abusive relationship
should seek help immediately. It can only be remedied by outside
assistance, possibly from a priest, minister, or counselor. Most
importantly though, help should be sought through prayer for as St.
Paul says, "For our wrestling is not against flesh and blood; but
against principalities and power, against the rulers of the world of
this darkness, against the spirits of wickedness in the high places."[72]

Our Father, Hail Mary, Glory Be, Etc.
Additional clause: ...of thy womb, Jesus,
who was scourged for our offenses.

119

The Crowning with Thorns

And the soldiers platting a crown of thorns, put it upon his head; and they put on him a purple garment. And they came to him, and said: Hail, king of the Jews; and they gave him blows.

For this cause shall a man leave his father and mother, and shall cleave to his wife, and they shall be two in one flesh.

- John 19:2-3, Ephesians 5:31

How many times have we heard wedding vows repeated? We may even be able to repeat our own vows from memory. Yet, how many of us consciously try to stick closely and apply ourselves to the vows we've made? Are we seeking to love our spouse when we do not treat him or her as a beautiful gift given to us by God? We are told to love our neighbors as ourselves. What closer neighbor is there than the one beside us in our bed? Yet, many times we go to bed angry and without speaking. Are we seeking to honor our spouse when we speak unkind words about them to our friends and family? To honor each other means to hold our spouse in high esteem. This may be difficult in some situations. However, if we keep our negative thoughts and feelings to ourselves and pray to overcome them we will honor our spouse. We honor each other by placing our husband or wife's needs before our own.

Jesus wore the crown of thorns that we deserve for our not keeping true to our marriage vows. The crown was pushed into his head for our sins of commission as well as omission. Let us strive to love, honor, and obey our spouse from this day forward.

Our Father, Hail Mary, Glory Be, Etc.
Additional clause: ...of thy womb, Jesus,
who was crowned with thorns.

The Carrying of the Cross

Then therefore he delivered him to them to be crucified.
And they took Jesus, and led him forth. And bearing his own cross,
he went forth to that place which is called Calvary, but in Hebrew
Golgotha.

For the word of the cross, to them indeed that perish, is
foolishness; but to them that are saved, that is, to us, it is the
power of God.

- John 19:16-17, 1 Corinthians 1:18

To those without faith the cross can appear as a condemnation.
They ask, "why not just put it down and move on"? They do not
realize that it is not condemnation but our salvation to pick up that
cross daily and follow Him.

At the altar we promised to love our spouse in the good times and
through the bad. In sickness and in health, for rich or for poor until
death do us part. According to God's plan, seemingly bad things
happen to good people. God often gives us an extremely heavy
cross to bear and that cross can sometimes be our spouse. A
permanent physical disability can make one spouse completely
dependent on the other. Sickness and disease can require life long
care. Mental disorders can make a spouse almost unlovable. It is
during these times, whether they be one year or one hundred years,
that we must fully conform ourselves to Christ. When our spouse
is the cross we bear daily, we must embrace that cross lovingly and
wholeheartedly. Jesus died for His spouse, the Church.

The spouse that feels he or she is a cross must not see themselves
as a condemnation but rather an instrument of salvation. God uses
all things for good for those who love Him and we are all Christ
and cross to each other.

The perfect picture of married life is the crucifix. Love married to
sacrifice. Suffering for the sake of another. The cross is useless
without Christ and there is no sacrifice for Christ without the cross.

Let us therefore die to our own wants and desires so that we may better love and care for our spouse. We have made vows to do this before God and His Church. Let us resolve to keep these vows no matter how many times we may fall under the weight of our cross. Let us stand once again and continue our journey together towards the kingdom.

Our Father, Hail Mary, Glory Be, Etc.
Additional clause: ...of thy womb, Jesus,
who carries the cross before us.

The Crucifixion and Death

When Jesus therefore had seen his mother and the disciple standing whom he loved, he saith to his mother: Woman, behold thy son. After that, he saith to the disciple: Behold thy mother. And from that hour, the disciple took her to his own. Jesus therefore, when he had taken the vinegar, said: It is consummated. And bowing his head, he gave up the ghost.

Now the mother was to be admired above measure, and worthy to be remembered by good men,... She said to them: I know not how you were formed in my womb; for I neither gave you breath, nor soul, nor life, neither did I frame the limbs of every one of you. But the Creator of the world, that formed the nativity of man, and that found out the origin of all, he will restore to you again, in his mercy, both breath and life

- John 19:26-27, 30, 2 Maccabees 7: 21,23

Till death do us part. It is not something we think about or look forward to. It is like an add-on or legal disclaimer at the bottom of the page we would rather not discuss. Death comes to us all. The loss of a spouse can be a devastating event in one's life regardless of the amount of time married. Like those followers gathered at the foot of the cross, many feelings and emotions come to the surface: sorrow for our loss; anger, because we somehow feel cheated; guilt, from not saying or doing something when we had the chance; fear of the future alone; so many feelings and emotions to deal with not to mention funeral arrangements, insurance, and more.

It is at this time when we must turn to the Mother of Sorrows for comfort. Like John, we must take her into our own home. We must sit with her and share our sorrows and fears. She understands. She has experienced loss. She will give us strength, encouragement, and hope. She will stand with us at the cross and guide us to the empty tomb. "I will deliver them out of the hand of death. I will redeem them from death: O death, I will be thy death; O hell, I will be thy bite..."[73]

Our Father, Hail Mary, Glory Be, Etc.
Additional clause: ...of thy womb, Jesus,
who gave us His Mother to comfort us.

The Glorious Mysteries of Marriage

The Resurrection

*Now when it was late that same day, the first of the week,
and the doors were shut, where the disciples were gathered
together, for fear of the Jews, Jesus came and stood in the midst,
and said to them: Peace be to you. And when he had said this, he
shewed them his hands and his side. The disciples therefore were
glad, when they saw the Lord.*

*For you are bought with a great price. Glorify and bear
God in your body.*

- John 20:19-20, 1 Corinthians 6:20

St. Paul tells us that the body is the temple of the Holy Spirit.[74]
We are to respect our own bodies as well as the body of our
spouse. The Resurrection reminds us that the body we possess
now is the one we will have forever. Many times we get caught up
in the fanciful notion that we will spend eternity as shapeless free-
floating spirits. The Resurrection teaches us that this is not true
and that one-day we will be reunited with our bodies.

If our body and soul are so closely connected it is only fitting that
we heed St. Paul's advice. "So also ought men to love their wives
as their own bodies. He that loveth his wife, loveth himself. For
no man ever hated his own flesh; but nourisheth and cherisheth it,
as also Christ doth the Church."

As a married couple we are one body, one flesh. Let us therefore
love and respect each other's bodies in a way that glorifies and
gives honor to God. Let us also use our bodies in this life to
sanctify each other and bring each other that much closer to a
resurrection into eternal life. "The wife hath not power of her own
body, but the husband. And in like manner the husband also hath
not power of his own body, but the wife."[75]

125

Our Father, Hail Mary, Glory Be, Etc.
Additional clause: ...of thy womb, Jesus,
who will call us to the resurrection of the body.

The Ascension

But you shall receive the power of the Holy Ghost coming
upon you, and you shall be witnesses unto me in Jerusalem, and in
all Judea, and Samaria, and even to the uttermost part of the earth.
And when he had said these things, while they looked on, he was
raised up: and a cloud received him out of their sight.
Lift up your gates, O ye princes, and be ye lifted up, O
eternal gates: and the King of Glory shall enter in. Who is this
King of Glory? the Lord of hosts, he is the King of Glory.

- Acts of the Apostles 1:8-9, Psalm 23:9-10

A common cause of stress and even resentment within marriage is
spirituality. Many times one spouse grows spiritually with leaps
and bounds while the other's growth seems stagnant or even non-
existent. Because they are no longer two but one uneven growth
can strain the relationship.

God has designed marriage in such a way that spiritual growth is to
be complementing and continuous between a husband and wife.
We are to encourage one another. If one advances in the spiritual
life more than the other, this should not be a source of resentment.
Like a taller plant beside a shorter one it should challenge and
encourage the smaller one to reach higher.

We are to await the Lord together. We must help each other be
ready for when He comes again. Our job as a faithful, loving
spouse is to challenge and encourage our beloved in the spiritual
life so that when Christ returns He will find us both ready to greet
Him. "For the unbelieving husband is sanctified by the believing
wife; and the unbelieving wife is sanctified by the believing
husband..."[76]

Our Father, Hail Mary, Glory Be, Etc.
Additional clause: ...of thy womb, Jesus,
who will return in the same way He left.

The Descent of the Holy Spirit

*The former treatise I made, O Theophilus, of all things
which Jesus began to do and to teach, Until the day on which,
giving commandments by the Holy Ghost to the apostles whom he
had chosen, he was taken up. To whom also he showed himself
alive after his passion, by many proofs, for forty days appearing to
them, and speaking of the kingdom of God. And eating together
with them, he commanded them, that they should not depart from
Jerusalem, but should wait for the promise of the Father, which
you have heard (saith he) by my mouth.*

*And they cried to the Lord in their affliction: and he
delivered them out of their distresses. He sent his word, and
healed them: and delivered them from their destructions.*

- Acts of the Apostles 2:1-4, Psalm 106:19-20

Prayer is the life and breath of the soul. Prayer is also the life and
breath of a marriage. As Fr. Peyton always stated, "The family
that prays together, stays together". Christ taught us that, "where
two or three are gathered together in my name, there am I in the
midst of them."[77] When a married couple comes together in
prayer, Jesus is in their midst. To pray together as husband and
wife is to call upon the power of God. It is in essence a miniature
Pentecost. Our prayer as one spirit, one body, one mind, makes us
imitators of the Trinity.

Let us therefore gather often in our upper room, living room, or
bedroom for fervent prayer. Let us allow ourselves to be filled
with the Holy Spirit so that we may preach the Gospel through
word and deed to our family, friends, and neighbors. The Holy
Spirit comes forth as the fruit of our prayer empowering and
renewing our marriage. He proceeds from the Father and the Son,
from the husband and the wife, by the husband and the wife He is
worshipped and glorified. "But you shall receive the power of the
Holy Ghost coming upon you, and you shall be witnesses unto me
in Jerusalem, and in all Judea, and Samaria, and even to the
uttermost part of the earth. "[78]

128

Our Father, Hail Mary, Glory Be, Etc.
Additional clause: ...of thy womb, Jesus,
who sends forth His Spirit upon our marriage.

The Assumption of Mary

And the temple of God was opened in heaven: and the ark of his testament was seen in his temple, and there were lightnings, and voices, and an earthquake, and great hail. And a great sign appeared in heaven: A woman clothed with the sun, and the moon under her feet, and on her head a crown of twelve stars:

And when she was come out to him, they all blessed her with one voice, saying: Thou art the glory of Jerusalem, thou art the joy of Israel, thou art the honour of our people

- Revelation 11:19, 12:1,14 Judith 15:10

Like Mary there is no way for us to draw closer to God by our own power. It is God's grace that leads us or rather pulls us to Himself. This is why St. Augustine says, "Our hearts are restless until they rest in you O Lord". Likewise our marriage is restless until it rests in the Lord. Our marriage cannot achieve the sanctity for which it is designed on its own power. Married life cannot ascend to the lofty yet reachable ideals of marriage by anything we do except insofar as we cooperate with grace. Only through this cooperation can our marriage be taken higher and it can be "assumed" to the heights prepared by God for those in matrimonial bonds.

By following the humility and example of the Blessed Mother we will begin to cooperate with God's grace. His grace will draw us closer to each other and to Himself. "You have made us for yourself and our hearts are restless until they rest in you O Lord."

Our Father, Hail Mary, Glory Be, Etc.
Additional clause: ...of thy womb, Jesus,
who draws us, like Mary, to Himself.

The Coronation of Mary

And a great sign appeared in heaven: A woman clothed with the sun, and the moon under her feet, and on her head a crown of twelve stars

All the glory of the king's daughter is within in golden borders, Clothed round about with varieties. After her shall virgins be brought to the king: her neighbours shall be brought to thee. They shall be brought with gladness and rejoicing: they shall be brought into the temple of the king.

- Revelation 12:1, Psalm 44:106

The picture of the heavenly court, completed by the crowning of the Queen, is a picture of a perfect heavenly marriage. The King and Queen, Jesus and Mary, look down upon their home, the kingdom, and their children. This is a look of concern and care not of power and control. True authority and power comes from the willingness to serve.

The husband and wife too look with care and concern upon their home, future, and their children. Mary gives the perfect example of a loving wife. She is subordinate to Jesus who is the head of their "home". She trusts in His strength, power, and justice. Likewise a wife should be obedient to her husband, not in a servile way but in a childlike self-abandoning way. Mary also intercedes for others, pleads for mercy, and requests favors from Jesus. A wife too may speak to her husband for her children or others. She may also plead for mercy for those around her and request favors and blessings from her husband. In similar fashion the husband is to imitate Christ. For as St. Paul says, "husbands love your wives as Christ loved the Church". Jesus loved His bride, the Church, so much that He took her place on the cross. He died for His bride so that she might have eternal life.

Let us strengthen our marriage by looking to the example of Jesus and Mary. Let us seek to imitate them by serving each other and our family. Mary, Queen of our marriage, pray for us.

131

Our Father, Hail Mary, Glory Be, Etc.
Additional clause: ...of thy womb, Jesus,
who is King of our marriage and home.

The Mysteries of the Mass

"Have you ever thought how you would prepare yourself to receive Our Lord if you could go to Communion only once in your life?

We must be thankful to God that he makes it so easy for us to come to him; but we should show our gratitude by preparing ourselves to receive him very well."
- St. Josemaria Escriva   *The Forge # 828*

The Joyful Mysteries of the Mass

The Annunciation

And in the sixth month, the angel Gabriel was sent from God into a city of Galilee, called Nazareth, to a virgin espoused to a man whose name was Joseph, of the house of David; and the virgin's name was Mary. And the angel being come in, said unto her: Hail, full of grace, the Lord is with thee: blessed art thou among women.

Therefore the Lord himself shall give you a sign. Behold a virgin shall conceive, and bear a son and his name shall be called Emmanuel.

- Luke 1:26-28, Isaiah 7:1

When the angel visited Mary the miraculous happened. At Jesus' conception in Mary's womb "the word" as St. John says "was made flesh and dwelt among us". During the Mass the miraculous happens again. At the words of consecration the Word once again becomes flesh and dwells not only among us but in us. The bread, which earth has given and human hands have made, becomes the Bread of Life. The fruit of the vine becomes the Blood of the Lamb.

During the Mass I experience my own personal annunciation. As the angel said to Mary, "behold you shall conceive a son", the priest says to me, "behold, the Lamb of God". Mary said, "fiat", "be it done unto me according to thy word". I say, "I am not worthy that you should enter…, but only say the word and I shall be healed". At this moment I also cry out, "thy will be done on earth as it is in heaven". But maybe I should cry out, "thy will be done on earth as it is in heaven here at Mass".

Our Father, Hail Mary, Glory Be, Etc.
Additional clause: …of thy womb, Jesus,
who becomes flesh at the Mass.

134

The Visitation

And Mary rising up in those days, went into the hill country with haste into a city of Juda. And she entered into the house of Zachary, and saluted Elizabeth. And it came to pass, that when Elizabeth heard the salutation of Mary, the infant leaped in her womb. And Elizabeth was filled with the Holy Ghost. And Mary abode with her about three months; and she returned to her own house.

And David was afraid of the Lord that day, saying: How shall the ark of the Lord come to me? And the ark of the Lord abode in the house of Obededom the Gethite three months: and the Lord blessed Obededom, and all his household.

- Luke 1:39-41, 56, 2 Kings 6:9,11

At the end of Mass the priest or deacon says, "The mass has ended. Go in peace to love and serve the Lord". In the older Latin translation the priest says, "Ite Missa est", the Mass is. I must remember that the Mass never ends. It is to be continued the rest of the day Sunday, Monday and every hour of everyday of the week. After receiving Jesus in the Eucharist, I, like Mary, must go "with haste" into the world. By carrying Christ with haste throughout the week others will recognize Him in what I say and do and their homes and lives will be blessed.

I must also recognize the visitation within the Mass. Directly after the Annunciation, when the word becomes flesh on the altar, I experience my own Visitation. The priest raises Our Lord in the Blessed Sacrament and says, "Behold the Lamb of God who takes away the sins of the world. Happy are those who are called to the wedding feast of the Lamb". Here Christ comes with haste to me and I say, "at the sound of your greeting my heart leaped for joy. Lord, I am not worthy that You should come under my roof. Speak but the word and my soul will be healed".

Our Father, Hail Mary, Glory Be, Etc.
Additional clause: ...of thy womb, Jesus,

135

who comes to me with haste at Mass

The Nativity

And she brought forth her firstborn son, and wrapped him up in swaddling clothes, and laid him in a manger; because there was no room for them in the inn.

And the Lord said to Moses: Behold I will rain bread from heaven for you; let the people go forth, and gather what is sufficient for every day: that I may prove them whether they will walk in my law, or not.

- Luke 2:7, Exodus 16:4

A newborn child in a feeding trough for animals. A piece of bread and a cup of wine. Both God? "This saying is hard, and who can hear it?"[79] As the Nativity shows and the Mass reaffirms, God's ways are not our ways. To see God in that little child in the cave requires faith. To see God in the Eucharist requires faith as well. For this reason St. Paul tells me, "we walk by faith and not by sight".[80] If I have faith I will see Jesus in the Mass. He is present in His word through the reading of the Scriptures. He is present in the person of the priest who acts *in persona Christi*, as another Christ. He is present in His body, the Church, gathered together to worship in spirit and in truth. It is easy to see Christ in these aspects of the Mass. However, it is difficult to see Him where He is most fully present in the Eucharist.

Lord, give me the eyes of faith to see you in the Mass. Help me to see you in the Eucharist and believe, "faith will tell [me] Christ is present when the feeble senses fail."[81] "Blessed are they that have not seen, and have believed."[82]

Our Father, Hail Mary, Glory Be, Etc.
Additional clause: ...of thy womb, Jesus,
who is the Bread of Life.

137

The Presentation

And he came by the Spirit into the temple. And when his parents brought in the child Jesus, to do for him according to the custom of the law, he also took him into his arms

But Melchisedech, the king of Salem, bringing forth bread and wine, for he was the priest of the most high God, blessed him, and said: Blessed be Abram by the most high God, who created heaven and earth.

-Luke 2:27-28a, Genesis 14:18-19

Simeon had waited his entire life to hold Jesus in his hands. At the Presentation Mary offers Jesus to Simeon who in turn offers Jesus to God. Simeon, in the priestly office, offers to God the Lamb according to the Mosaic Law.[83]

As a baptized Catholic, Christ is present in me and I have become part of His mystical body. At Mass, I, like Jesus, am offered through the intercession of Mary to the priest. I should not simply show up and attend Mass. I am supposed to bring my entire life and all that I am. I should bring my sorrow, joy, pain, family, work, and every other aspect of my life to give to God as an offering. This offering is symbolized by the bread, wine, and money or other offering that comes not from my surplus but from my need.

When I bring each part of my life to Mass and join it to the life of every other person we become that mystical body truly present in the Church. God looks with love on His only Son, Jesus, as the head and His body, the Church. The priest says to me as Simeon said of Jesus, "behold, you are set for the fall and the resurrection of many and you will leave this Mass and be a sign of contradiction to the world and I reply, "Amen! Amen!"

Our Father, Hail Mary, Glory Be, Etc.
Additional clause: ...of thy womb, Jesus,
who is offered by the priest to God.

The Finding in the Temple

And not finding him, they returned into Jerusalem, seeking him. And it came to pass, that, after three days, they found him in the temple, sitting in the midst of the doctors, hearing them, and asking them questions.

He will guide the mild in judgment: he will teach the meek his ways.

...and a little child shall lead them.

- Luke 2:45-46, Psalm 24:9, Isaiah 11:6d

I come to Mass to find the answers to the questions concerning life. God can teach me through my questions in the same way the boy Jesus taught the elders in the Temple by asking them questions. If going to Mass is simply a fulfillment of an obligation there is no reason to go. The Mass is where I find Jesus. I find Him there teaching and asking me questions.

I am weak and in the time between Masses I often lose sight of Christ. The devil always tries to tempt me away from Christ regardless of whether I assist at Mass daily or once a week. Then all at once I notice, like Mary and Joseph, that I have left Christ somewhere behind me. That is why I must return to Mass as quickly as possible. Mary and Joseph did not waste any time. Scripture says, "they returned to Jerusalem seeking Him."

I too must adopt this sense of urgency and return to Mass as often as my state in life will allow. I am sure to find Him in weekly or daily Eucharistic celebration. When I do find Him I will understand that He is always waiting for me at Mass. And after I receive Him in the Eucharist, *I* will grow in wisdom, and age, and grace with God and man.[84]

Our Father, Hail Mary, Glory Be, Etc.
Additional clause: ...of thy womb, Jesus,
who is waiting to teach me at Mass

139

The Luminous Mysteries of the Mass

The Baptism of Jesus

And Jesus being baptized, forthwith came out of the water: and lo, the heavens were opened to him: and he saw the Spirit of God descending as a dove, and coming upon him. And behold a voice from heaven, saying: This is my beloved Son, in whom I am well pleased.

They shall no more hunger nor thirst, neither shall the sun fall on them, nor any heat. For the Lamb, which is in the midst of the throne, shall rule them, and shall lead them to the fountains of the waters of life, and God shall wipe away all tears from their eyes.

- Matt 3:16-17, Revelation 7:16-17

Jesus sanctified the waters of baptism by being baptized in the Jordan by John. I am reminded of my baptismal promises before the Mass begins as I enter the church. The water in the holy water font serves as a reminder that I have renounced sin, died with Christ, and will one day come out of the waters of death to eternal life. I, as a baptized Catholic, believe that the Mass is truly heaven on earth and since Scripture tells me that nothing unclean can enter heaven I wash myself before entering the heavenly banquet.

Water is an integral part of the Mass from the crossing of myself with holy water and washing of the priest's hands to the water mixed with wine before the consecration. This water should always remind me of my baptism in Christ who is the Living Water. It should also remind me of the water and blood that flowed forth from the Savior's side giving birth to the Church.

Lord, help me to remember my promise to renounce Satan and all his works as I wash myself in preparation for the Holy Banquet. Help me also to remember that in receiving the cup I not only drink the Blood of Our Lord but the blood and water that gushed forth at the birth of the Church. *Blood of Christ, inebriate me. Water from the side of Christ, wash me.*[85]

Our Father, Hail Mary, Glory Be, Etc.
Additional clause: ...of thy womb, Jesus,
who washes me clean at Mass.

The Wedding at Cana

And when the chief steward had tasted the water made wine, and knew not whence it was, but the waiters knew who had drawn the water; the chief steward calleth the bridegroom, And saith to him: Every man at first setteth forth good wine, and when men have well drunk, then that which is worse. But thou hast kept the good wine until now. This beginning of miracles did Jesus in Cana of Galilee; and manifested his glory, and his disciples believed in him.

And he took the blood and sprinkled it upon the people, and he said: This is the blood of the covenant, which the Lord hath made with you concerning all these words.

- John 2:9-11, Exodus 24:8

The Wedding at Cana offers so much for meditation on the Mass. Jesus worked His first miracle here at this wedding feast. Many times throughout the Gospel Jesus refers to heaven as a wedding feast or a wedding banquet. The book of Revelation ends triumphantly with the wedding feast of the Lamb. The holy sacrifice of the Mass is in fact this wedding feast described in the book of Revelation. It is the celebration and consummation of the marriage of Christ and His Church. At Mass we recite our vows with the Creed thereby proclaiming our undying love for our spouse, Jesus. He consummates the marriage by giving us, His bride, the Church, His very flesh for the life of the world.

At the Wedding at Cana Jesus changed ordinary water into exceptional wine. At the holy sacrifice of the Mass, Jesus, acting through the person of the priest, changes ordinary wine into His precious Blood, the Blood of the Lamb.

Lord, help me to celebrate this mystical marriage to Christ more reverently and more fervently at every Mass. Help me to put on my wedding garment and wash it in the Blood of the Lamb poured out for me at every Mass.

Our Father, Hail Mary, Glory Be, Etc.
Additional clause: ...of thy womb, Jesus,
who changes wine into His own Blood.

The Proclamation of the Kingdom

The time is accomplished, and the kingdom of God is at hand: repent, and believe the gospel.

And the seventh angel sounded the trumpet: and there were great voices in heaven, saying: The kingdom of this world is become our Lord's and his Christ's, and he shall reign for ever and ever. Amen.

- Mark 1:15, Revelation 11:15

Every Mass is an apocalypse which in Greek means an "unveiling". It is an unveiling of the great mystery of the Kingdom. For those who have eyes to see and those who have ears to hear, Heaven is unveiled and the Kingdom is revealed in the Mass. When Jesus began His ministry he began with these words, "Repent, for the Kingdom of God is at hand."[86] These words should echo loudly as I prepare to participate at Mass. The Kingdom of God is at hand but most especially and most fully in the Mass.

I must repent, as Jesus says, before I enter into the Kingdom and for this reason the Church places the penitential rite at the beginning of the Mass. Otherwise I am, as Saint Paul says, "guilty of the body and blood of the Lord." This means that I am guilty of causing His death because of my unwillingness to repent. Repent, for the Kingdom of God is at hand at Mass.

Our Father, Hail Mary, Glory Be, Etc.
Additional clause: ...of thy womb, Jesus, who calls me to repentance.

144

The Transfiguration

*And after six days Jesus taketh with him Peter and James
and John, and leadeth them up into a high mountain apart by
themselves, and was transfigured before them. And his garments
became shining and exceeding white as snow, so as no fuller upon
earth can make white. And there appeared to them Elias with
Moses; and they were talking with Jesus.*

*Moses did not know that the skin of his face shone because
he had been talking with God.*

Mark 9:1-3, Exodus 34:29b(RSV)

The Transfiguration is the revelation of God's glory physically
manifested in Jesus. In this event I see Jesus speaking with Moses
and Elijah. These two men represent the Old Testament Law and
Prophets respectively. "The New Testament lies hidden in the Old
and the Old Testament is unveiled in the New."[87]

In the Mass I receive Christ in two concrete ways. I receive Him
physically: Body, Blood, Soul, and Divinity in the Eucharist. I
also receive Him just as concretely in the Liturgy of the Word.
The reading of Scripture is not just an old tradition of the Church.
Nor is the reading of scripture a lead-in for the priest's homily.
The reading of scripture is an integral part of the liturgy. In it I
receive the very words of God written under the inspiration of the
Holy Spirit. In the light of Scripture I see that all revelation points
to and finds its source in Jesus Christ. When I begin to see Jesus in
both the Liturgy of the Word and the Liturgy of the Eucharist I,
like Peter, will say, "It is good for us to be here." It is good for me
to be here, at Mass.

Our Father, Hail Mary, Glory Be, Etc.
Additional clause: ...of thy womb, Jesus,
who is truly present at Mass.

The Institution of the Eucharist

And taking bread, he gave thanks, and brake; and gave to them, saying: This is my body, which is given for you. Do this for a commemoration of me. In like manner the chalice also, after he had supped, saying: This is the chalice, the new testament in my blood, which shall be shed for you.

And it shall be a lamb without blemish, a male, of one year; according to which rite also you shall take a kid. And thus you shall eat it: you shall gird your reins, and you shall have shoes on your feet, holding staves in your hands, and you shall eat in haste; for it is the Phase (that is the Passage) of the Lord. And this day shall be for a memorial to you; and you shall keep it a feast to the Lord in your generations, with an everlasting observance.

- Luke 22:19-20, Exodus 12:5, 11,14

The Eucharist is the source and summit of the Christian life.[88] In the Eucharist I find my strength.

At the Last Supper Jesus gave Himself to His apostles in a real, physical way under the appearance of bread and wine. It was not merely a symbolic act but a real event intended to replace the very event they were commemorating.

I often confuse my understanding of the word remember and commemorate with the understanding of those words in the time of Christ. To "remember" did not mean to simply look back fondly on an event somewhere in history. It meant to make that event present again in the here and now. The Mass is not a fond feel-good-pretend-time re-enactment of the Last Supper. It is a re-presentation of the same events that took place over two thousand years ago in an unbloody manner.

I could not be there in the Upper Room or on Calvary so God, who is beyond time, makes this one sacrifice present to me. The Mass is the new Passover. It is the New Covenant in which the spotless

Lamb is offered as a sacrifice for the sins of God's family thus protecting them from eternal death. At every Mass it is the same Lamb, Jesus. It is the same sacrifice, Calvary. "From the rising of the sun even to the going down... and in every place there is sacrifice, and there is offered to my name a clean oblation."[89]

Our Father, Hail Mary, Glory Be, Etc.
Additional clause: ...of thy womb, Jesus,
who gives me Himself in the Eucharist.

The Sorrowful Mysteries of the Mass

The Agony in the Garden

And he was withdrawn away from them a stone's cast; and kneeling down, he prayed, saying: Father, if thou wilt, remove this chalice from me: but yet not my will, but thine be done. And his sweat became as drops of blood, trickling down upon the ground.

And he said to me: My grace is sufficient for thee; for power is made perfect in infirmity. Gladly therefore will I glory in my infirmities, that the power of Christ may dwell in me.

- Luke 22:41-42,44, 2Corinthians 12:9

Jesus asked that the cup pass Him by. This cup was the cup of suffering and death. In His agony He saw what He was to suffer for my sake and the sight caused Him to sweat drops of blood. The Blood of Christ and the cup are set before me at Mass. Jesus asked His followers, "can you drink the chalice that I shall drink?" To drink from the cup means to share in Christ's Blood. To drink from the cup means to share in Christ's suffering as well. As I kneel and listen to the words of consecration and the priest lifts high the chalice I must remember that to share in the cup means to share in the suffering. By proclaiming the death of the Lord Jesus by eating "this bread and drinking this cup" I unite myself fully to the life of Christ including suffering. From my humble position on my knees I must learn to say, "not my will Father, but thine be done." I must learn to receive this cup and willingly share in the sufferings of Jesus as St. Paul says, "... I Paul am made a minister. Who now rejoice in my sufferings for you, and fill up those things that are wanting of the sufferings of Christ, in my flesh, for his body, which is the church."[90]

Our Father, Hail Mary, Glory Be, Etc.
Additional clause: ...of thy womb, Jesus,
who drank from the cup of suffering.

148

The Scourging at the Pillar

Then cried they all again, saying: Not this man, but Barabbas. Now Barabbas was a robber. Then therefore, Pilate took Jesus, and scourged him.

Confess therefore your sins one to another: and pray one for another, that you may be saved. For the continual prayer of a just man availeth much.

- John 18:40-19:1, James 5:16

With each lash of the whip extreme pain coursed through Our Savior's body. His flesh was torn open and His back was scarred and bloody. However, when He was given a cloak and shown to the people His wounds were not visible even though the pain was still there. Scripture tells us that, "by His bruises we are healed."[91] The body of Our Lord was wounded for our sins and continues to be even today. For as Our Lord tells Saul, soon to be Paul, "I am Jesus whom thou persecutest."[92]

Like the scars on Jesus' back my sufferings are not always visible. At Mass I am to bring my entire life including my sufferings and place them on the altar before God to be healed. As I stand gathered with the body of Christ, the Church, I must learn to look at the back of the person before me and see the sufferings they carry. I do not know what scars and sufferings they may carry but I can help them to be healed by praying for them at Mass.

Lord, help me to remember my neighbors before, behind, and beside me and present their needs and sufferings as well as my own to You through Your Son. The Church is one body in Christ. It is "Jesus and we", not "Jesus and me."

Our Father, Hail Mary, Glory Be, Etc.
Additional clause: ...of thy womb, Jesus,
who was scourged for our offenses.

149

The Crowning with Thorns

And the soldiers platting a crown of thorns, put it upon his head; and they put on him a purple garment. And they came to him, and said: Hail, king of the Jews; and they gave him blows.

And they brought out the king's son, and put the crown upon him, and the testimony, and gave him the law to hold in his hand, and they made him king...

-John 19:2-3, 2 Chronicles 23:11a

Without the proper knowledge and instruction on the beauty of the Mass my mind can wander easily. I can be distracted by the family that always arrives just before the reading of the Gospel. My mind can begin to wander when the priest fails to grab my attention with a riveting homily. A screaming infant or playful toddler can easily draw me "out of" the Mass. It is during these tempting times that I must remember Jesus' crowning with thorns. His focus was not on what the soldiers were wearing. He wasn't judging them because He saw them stumble out of the pub the night before. With each blow to His head He focused more intently on me. Everything He was enduring was for me and because of me; my face was constantly before Him. As His vision blurred from the blood running into His eyes, He simply closed them in order to see me better.

At Mass my focus should always be on Jesus. If my mind begins to wander or become distracted I should simply close my eyes to "see" Him better.

Lord, help me to recommit myself at Mass with a conscious effort to focus more on Jesus, the head crowned with thorns, and not the body, the Church, around me.

Our Father, Hail Mary, Glory Be, Etc.
Additional clause: ...of thy womb, Jesus,
who was crowned with thorns.

The Carrying of the Cross

And bearing his own cross, he went forth to that place which is called Calvary, but in Hebrew Golgotha.

And as they led him away, they laid hold of one Simon of Cyrene, coming from the country; and they laid the cross on him to carry after Jesus.

Jesus is entered for us, made a high priest for ever according to the order of Melchisedech.

- John 19:17, Luke 23:26, Hebrews 6:20b

Each person has his own cross to carry and Jesus asks me to pick mine up daily and follow Him. The priest has an enormous cross to carry. He, like Jesus, is often seen as the only sinful person in a world of holy men and women. For some priests it is as though they can do nothing that will please their parishioners.

I must remember to pray for all priests at Mass. They carry a cross that is very different from mine. They carry their cross to the altar at every Mass. They carry the nagging parishioner, monthly bills, troubled marriages, and my sins from the confessional and lay them on the altar before the Lord.

Instead of being Pilate, a soldier, or a Pharisee to my priest I must become Simon of Cyrene. I must learn to offer myself and my talents to help him carry his cross. If I am willing to do this, my priest will be better able to offer the sacraments. He will be better able to offer the sacrifice of the Mass. If my priest is "in persona Christi" another Christ, I can be another Simon.

Our Father, Hail Mary, Glory Be, Etc.
Additional clause: ...of thy womb, Jesus,
who is present in my priest.

The Crucifixion and Death

It is consummated. And bowing his head, he gave up the ghost. But after they were come to Jesus, when they saw that he was already dead, they did not break his legs.

And it shall be a lamb without blemish, a male, And they shall eat the flesh that night

And I, if I be lifted up from the earth, will draw all things to myself.

- John 19:30b, 33; Exodus 12:5a, 8a; John 12:32

"I will draw all things to myself." As the priest "lifts up" the consecrated host and chalice, he says or sings, "Through Him, with Him, in him. In the unity of the Holy Spirit all glory and honor are yours Almighty Father, for ever and ever." At this moment, when Christ is lifted up, He indeed draws all things to Himself. God the Father sees all of creation through His Son by the power of the Holy Spirit. At this moment during the Mass Jesus draws the Church to Himself and gives His flesh to His bride, the Church. God the Father sees His Son in Jesus, the head, and the Church, His body.

During this elevation of Jesus I should hear in the background the words of Jesus in the seventeenth chapter of John. A few verses will not suffice. The chapter should be read in its entirety. It is Christ's prayer for His Church. Through the sacrifice of the Lamb of God upon the altar of the cross we are reunited through the Son to the Father. Through that same sacrifice at each and every Mass we become one body in Christ.

Lord, when you look upon me at Mass you see your Son. Help me to more fully conform myself to His image and likeness by receiving Him in the Eucharist. Help me to avoid sin and confess often so that when your Son is lifted up and draws all things to Himself you will see a pure offering without blemish.

Our Father, Hail Mary, Glory Be, Etc.

Additional clause: ...of thy womb, Jesus,
who was lifted up on the cross to draw us to Himself.

The Glorious Mysteries of the Mass

The Resurrection

For I know that my Redeemer liveth, and in the last day I shall rise out of the earth. And I shall be clothed again with my skin, and in my flesh I shall see my God.

And it came to pass, whilst he was at table with them, he took bread, and blessed, and brake, and gave to them. And their eyes were opened, and they knew him: and he vanished out of their sight.

- Job 19:25-26, Luke 24:30-31

After the Resurrection, Jesus appeared to the disciples walking on the road to Emmaus. He spoke with them while they walked and explained the Scriptures. This Gospel account is a mirror image of my life. I, like the disciples, get discouraged and downhearted on my walk through life. Promises and ideas that once filled my heart with joy have been cast into the shadows of my mind. The coming of the Lord appears to be far off and sadness and despair creep into my life. I often make my way through the week with my head down kicking stones.

However, I must remember that Jesus walks with me even though I may not recognize Him. When I make the Mass part of my daily walk, my life changes. At Mass Jesus opens the Scriptures to me and my heart begins to burn within me. Even though I may not always recognize Him in the Scriptures, in the breaking of the bread my eyes are opened. I may not see Him in a physical human form but He is there in the breaking of the bread. In fact He is the Bread. Once I recognize Him I am able to "rise up that same hour" and say to the world, "The Lord is risen indeed!"

Our Father, Hail Mary, Glory Be, Etc.
Additional clause: ...of thy womb, Jesus,
who is present in the breaking of the bread.

154

The Ascension

Going therefore, teach ye all nations; baptizing them in the name of the Father, and of the Son, and of the Holy Ghost. Teaching them to observe all things whatsoever I have commanded you: and behold I am with you all days, even to the consummation of the world.

God is ascended with jubilee, and the Lord with the sound of trumpet.

- Matt 28:19-20, Psalm 46:6

Jesus ascended into heaven yet He remains with us. How can this be? With God all things are possible. He has indeed ascended and sits at the right hand of the Father. He has ascended in His human body. However, He remains with us "even until the end of the age." He remains with us most fully at Mass. He is truly present in the people, the Scriptures, His priest, and most especially in the Eucharist.

God fed His people in the desert wilderness with manna each and every day. He fed them with bread from heaven and sustained them throughout their journey. I too am on a journey toward the land promised to my fathers for generations. On this pilgrimage through the desert, the time between Christ's Ascension and return, I am sustained by the true Bread come down from heaven. I am sustained by the heavenly manna, the Bread of Life, given to me at each Mass.

Lord, I know you will return in the same way as you left. Therefore, whenever I eat this Bread and drink this Cup, I will proclaim your death Lord Jesus, at every Mass, until You come in glory. Maranatha, Come Lord Jesus.

Our Father, Hail Mary, Glory Be, Etc.
Additional clause: ...of thy womb, Jesus,
who feeds me on my journey.

The Descent of the Holy Spirit

*And suddenly there came a sound from heaven, as of a
mighty wind coming, and it filled the whole house where they were
sitting. And there appeared to them parted tongues as it were of
fire, and it sat upon every one of them: And they were all filled
with the Holy Ghost, and they began to speak with divers tongues,
according as the Holy Ghost gave them to speak. Now there were
dwelling at Jerusalem, Jews, devout men, out of every nation under
heaven. But others mocking, said: These men are full of new wine.*

*...since you are eager for manifestations of the Spirit, strive
to excel in building up the church.*

- Acts 2:2-5, 13, 1 Corinthians 14:12(RSV)

The reaction of one who is not Catholic to the events of the Mass is
oftentimes the same reaction exhibited by those who were outside
the Upper Room during Pentecost. The inability to see the power
of the Mass can confuse and offend many. Each Mass is a
miniature Pentecost. There is a gathering of the followers of Christ
in one place and, like the apostles, they are committing themselves
to prayer, being of one mind. The power of the Holy Spirit courses
through the priest and the people as they celebrate the Eucharist.

I need to be more like Peter and proclaim the Gospel with wild
abandon and not abandon the Gospel as I exit the Church door.
My zeal should cause people to accuse me of being drunk because
I am inebriated with the Truth I have received at Mass. When I
finally realize the power of the Mass, people will be coming and
asking what they should do in order to be saved after hearing me
speak when I leave Mass.

Lord, give me a fuller outpouring of the Spirit that I may give
fearless witness to Your Gospel. Help me to realize the full power
of the Mass and take that power into my home, my community,
and the world. "It is no longer I that live but Christ that lives in
me."[93]

Our Father, Hail Mary, Glory Be, Etc.
Additional clause: ...of thy womb, Jesus,
who sends the Holy Spirit at Mass.

The Assumption of Mary

And there were given to the woman two wings of a great eagle, that she might fly into the desert unto her place, where she is nourished for a time and times, and half a time, from the face of the serpent.

All the glory of the king's daughter is within in golden borders, Clothed round about with varieties. After her shall virgins be brought to the king: her neighbours shall be brought to thee. They shall be brought with gladness and rejoicing: they shall be brought into the temple of the king.

Revelation 12:14, Psalm 44:14-16

I cannot move towards God unless He moves toward me first. It is His grace that calls me to love Him. At the beginning of the Eucharistic prayer during Mass we say, "we lift them [our hearts] up to the Lord." This is in response to the Lord's invitation through His priest to, "lift up your hearts."

In Scripture Mary is often seen as a symbol or sign of the Church. In the Assumption I see the Mass. I see the assumption of the Church into heaven. Because the Church is composed of imperfect people, it can only "lift up her heart". In response to this "offering" heaven comes to earth on the altar. On the altar of sacrifice, at every Mass, there is an assumption. The Church is assumed by the power of God into heaven.

Through Him, with Him, in Him, in the unity of the Holy Spirit the Church is assumed at each Mass to the glory and honor of the Almighty Father forever and ever. On the altar, heaven and earth embrace. Mercy and truth have met each other: "justice and peace have kissed."[94]

Our Father, Hail Mary, Glory Be, Etc.
Additional clause: ...of thy womb, Jesus,
who lifts me up to the Lord.

158

The Coronation of Mary

And a great sign appeared in heaven: A woman clothed with the sun, and the moon under her feet, and on her head a crown of twelve stars

One is my dove, my perfect one is but one, she is the only one of her mother, the chosen of her that bore her. The daughters saw her, and declared her most blessed: the queens and concubines, and they praised her.

- Revelation 12:1, Song of Songs 6:8

The Blessed Virgin Mary is a symbol and sign of the Church. In this meditation I see not only Mary as Queen of Heaven and Earth but also the Church as Queen of Heaven and Earth. I also see the Church as mother here on earth. Like a natural mother she nurtures and feeds her offspring from her own body. She feeds her offspring most fully at the Mass. Her children are fed with the very word of God in the Liturgy of the Word. They are fed with her very body, that is, Christ in the flesh, in the Liturgy of the Eucharist.

I must remember that when I am assisting at Mass I am in the womb of my mother, the Church. I am being nourished on the word, scripture, and the Word made flesh, the Eucharist, so that I may emerge, born anew in spirit to bring light and life to the world.

In order for me to be a true son of the Father and a brother of Christ I must love and respect my mother the Church. Christ gives me help in learning to love the Church by giving me His own Mother to love. In loving Mary I will learn to love the Church. In loving Mary I will learn to love the Mass. Queen of Heaven and Earth, pray for us.

Our Father, Hail Mary, Glory Be, Etc.
Additional clause: ...of thy womb, Jesus,
who gave me His Mother and the Church.

159

First Person Mysteries of the Rosary

> *"Sine me nihil potestis facere!"* – "Without me you can do nothing!" New light – new splendor – for my eyes, from the eternal light, the holy Gospel.
>
> Now should I be surprised at all of "my" foolishness?
>
> Let me put Jesus into everything that is mine; then there will be no foolishness in my conduct. And if I would speak correctly, I would talk no more of what is "mine", but of what is "ours".

- St. Josemaria Escriva   *The Way # 416*

The Joyful Mysteries through the eyes of St. Joseph

The Annunciation

Mary was espoused to Joseph, before they came together, she was found with child, of the Holy Ghost. Whereupon Joseph her husband, being a just man, and not willing publicly to expose her, was minded to put her away privately. But while he thought on these things, behold the angel of the Lord appeared to him in his sleep, saying: Joseph, son of David, fear not to take unto thee Mary thy wife, for that which is conceived in her, is of the Holy Ghost. And she shall bring forth a son: and thou shalt call his name JESUS. For he shall save his people from their sins.

- Matthew 1:18-21

When Mary told me she was with child I didn't know what to say. I didn't know what to think. I felt betrayed and angry yet I did not want her to receive the punishment called for by the Law. Later that evening I decided to divorce her quietly when an angel appeared and spoke to me. I was amazed and thought I was dreaming. The next day I told Mary about the dream. Only then did she tell me her side of the story. She told me how an angel had appeared to her also and told her things that were similar to what the angel had told me in my dream. I asked her why she didn't tell me this before. She said that she knew the Lord would provide my answer in His own way and she didn't want to interfere. That is just like her, always leaving everything to the Lord.

Our Father, Hail Mary, Glory Be, Etc.
Additional clause: ...of thy womb, Jesus,
who was conceived by the Holy Spirit.

161

The Visitation

And Mary said: My soul doth magnify the Lord. And my spirit hath rejoiced in God my Saviour. Because he hath regarded the humility of his handmaid; for behold from henceforth all generations shall call me blessed. Because he that is mighty, hath done great things to me; and holy is his name. And his mercy is from generation unto generations, to them that fear him. He hath shewed might in his arm: he hath scattered the proud in the conceit of their heart. He hath put down the mighty from their seat, and hath exalted the humble. He hath filled the hungry with good things; and the rich he hath sent empty away. He hath received Israel his servant, being mindful of his mercy: As he spoke to our fathers, to Abraham and to his seed for ever.

- Luke 1:46-55

When Mary told me she was going to visit her cousin in the hill country I was slightly worried. She told me not to worry and that I could visit when I had the time. Mary stayed with her cousin for about three months. I remember her coming home after that time and being so excited. She told me of how her cousins' child had leapt in the womb when she first arrived and at the sound of her greeting. She composed some poetry too while she was there and recited it for me while I worked on a table for our neighbor. I can't remember all the words but it was uplifting. I remember looking up from my work as she was reading. It was as if she were glowing. Her eyes were closed and it seemed as if she were speaking to God and not to me. Maybe she was.

Our Father, Hail Mary, Glory Be, Etc.
Additional clause: ...of thy womb, Jesus,
who caused John to leap in his mothers' womb.

The Nativity

*And there were in the same country shepherds watching,
and keeping the night watches over their flock. And behold an
angel of the Lord stood by them, and the brightness of God shone
round about them; and they feared with a great fear.*

*And this shall be a sign unto you. You shall find the infant
wrapped in swaddling clothes, and laid in a manger.*

Luke 2:8-9,12

It was the most difficult time in my life but also the most joyous. I
was dealing with so many emotions I didn't know where to turn. I
felt like the smallest man on the earth that night and then, later on,
the greatest.

We had to go back to the homeland for the census. When we
arrived it was horrible. There were families everywhere and no
room for more. Mary was expecting Jesus at any time and her
riding on the mule wasn't slowing the process any. I felt defeated
when I couldn't even find a comfortable room for her. We
wandered most of the night until I found an old cave that was
being used as a stable. It was dark and smelly but I managed to
find some clean bedding and fixed a place for Mary to lie down.
Of course, of all the times to have a child, this had to be the night.
I did all I could to help with the birth. After He was born, and
Mary was nursing the baby, I found a feeding trough and placed
some clean bedding in it for a crib and placed it beside Mary and
Jesus. I was exhausted by then and I had just sat down when the
owners of the stable returned. They weren't upset. Actually they
said that they hadn't planned on coming back for a few days but
they had been told to come back. They said angels had appeared to
them. I knew exactly how they felt. We watched as Mary and
Jesus slept peacefully

Our Father, Hail Mary, Glory Be, Etc.
Additional clause: ...of thy womb, Jesus,
who was born in a stable.

The Presentation

And behold there was a man in Jerusalem named Simeon, and this man was just and devout, waiting for the consolation of Israel; and the Holy Ghost was in him. And he had received an answer from the Holy Ghost, that he should not see death, before he had seen the Christ of the Lord. And he came by the Spirit into the temple. And when his parents brought in the child Jesus, to do for him according to the custom of the law, he also took him into his arms, and blessed God, and said: Now thou dost dismiss thy servant, O Lord, according to thy word in peace; Because my eyes have seen thy salvation, Which thou hast prepared before the face of all peoples: A light to the revelation of the Gentiles, and the glory of thy people Israel.

- Luke 2:28-32

I accompanied Mary to the temple for the purification that day. We were just about to enter the temple when an older gentleman approached. He asked us if he could hold the baby. He looked like a respectable man, a priest maybe, so we allowed him to hold Jesus. His gray eyes glowed as he lifted the child from his mothers' arms. He just held Jesus up at arms length and stared at Him for a very long time. I saw tears begin to form in his eyes as his beard broke open to reveal his smile. He began to speak about Jesus to us yet he never took his eyes off the child. He said some things that I thought might upset Mary but she just took it all in and smiled quietly.

Our Father, Hail Mary, Glory Be, Etc.
Additional clause: ...of thy womb, Jesus,
who was presented at the Temple.

The Finding in the Temple

And seeing him, they wondered. And his mother said to him: Son, why hast thou done so to us? behold thy father and I have sought thee sorrowing. And he said to them: How is it that you sought me? did you not know, that I must be about my father's business? And they understood not the word that he spoke unto them. And he went down with them, and came to Nazareth, and was subject to them. And his mother kept all these words in her heart. And Jesus advanced in wisdom, and age, and grace with God and men.

- Luke 2:48-52

We had been going to the Passover Feast every year but He had never done anything like this. We had been traveling home with all of our relatives when we discovered that Jesus was missing. We thought He was with the other children in the group but they said that they hadn't seen Him since we left Jerusalem. No one else had seen Him either so we headed back to Jerusalem. I was upset and worried but Mary was just determined. She had no doubt that we would find Him. We did find Him yet it was a confusing situation. He was in the temple listening to the teachers of the Law and asking them questions. When Mary finally caught His attention and called Him over to question Him, He mentioned something about being in His Father's house. I felt the eyes of the Temple on us, I felt like they all knew that Jesus wasn't my child. I was confused but remained silent, in my heart He was always my child. I loved Him as if He were my own.

Our Father, Hail Mary, Glory Be, Etc.
Additional clause: ...of thy womb, Jesus,
who was found in the Temple.

The Luminous Mysteries through the eyes of Various People

The Baptism of Jesus – St. Andrew

*The next day again John stood, and two of his disciples.
And beholding Jesus walking, he saith: Behold the Lamb of God.
And the two disciples heard him speak, and they followed Jesus.
And Jesus turning, and seeing them following him, saith to them:
What seek you? Who said to him, Rabbi, (which is to say, being
interpreted, Master,) where dwellest thou? He saith to them:
Come and see.*

*And I saw that the Lamb had opened one of the seven seals,
and I heard one of the four living creatures, as it were the voice of
thunder, saying: Come, and see.*

- John 1:35-39, Revelation 6:1

I had been going to listen to John for a few months. I listened
every time I had a free moment. My brother thought I was crazy
and couldn't understand why anyone would listen to a crazy
preacher instead of fishing.

John had been preaching about repentance for as long as anyone
could remember. He had also been preaching about this person
who was to come after him yet this person was before him. The
story didn't make much sense at the time.

I was there when John baptized Jesus. John was standing in the
Jordan as usual with the water flowing just above his knees. He
was quite a sight with the camel hair cloak and long beard blowing
in the wind. It reminded me of Moses preparing to part the Red
Sea.

As Jesus approached, time appeared to stand still. The sky was
clear and there was not a sound to be heard. The river looked like

glass with John frozen in its midst. Then I heard John say in a voice that seemed to echo throughout creation, "Behold the Lamb of God who takes away the sins of the world". Jesus entered the river and was baptized by John. My friend and I decided to follow Jesus to find where He was staying. He noticed us following and recognized us from the river and said, "come, and see".

Our Father, Hail Mary, Glory Be, Etc.
Additional clause: ...of thy womb, Jesus,
who was baptized by John.

The Wedding at Cana – a Servant

And the wine failing, the mother of Jesus saith to him:
They have no wine. And Jesus saith to her: Woman, what is that to
me and to thee? my hour is not yet come. His mother saith to the
waiters: Whatsoever he shall say to you, do ye. Now there were
set there six waterpots of stone, according to the manner of the
purifying of the Jews, containing two or three measures apiece.
Jesus saith to them: Fill the waterpots with water. And they filled
them up to the brim. And Jesus saith to them: Draw out now, and
carry to the chief steward of the feast. And they carried it.

And no man putteth new wine into old bottles: otherwise
the wine will burst the bottles, and both the wine will be spilled,
and the bottles will be lost. But new wine must be put into new
bottles.

- John 2:3-8, Mark 2:22

It looked like disaster. The feast had just begun when the wine
began to disappear. Jesus' mother noticed my distress and pulled
me aside and I explained the situation. She motioned to Jesus and
He came and joined in the discussion. After a few moments, He
instructed me to fill the jars of purification with water. I did not
question His instructions because I was desperate and wanted to
keep my job. He then told me to take some of the water to my
boss.

I simply stood there for a moment with my mouth open. I thought
He was going to help me in some way but now I realized He was
sending me to the unemployment line. I dipped a pitcher in the
water but I never took my eyes off of Him. I couldn't believe what
He was asking me to do. Another servant and I walked slowly
toward the head-waiter. As I handed him the pitcher I began to
ponder where I might be working next. I felt myself becoming
angry with Jesus and set my mind to tell Him what I thought of
Him when I had the chance. The head-waiter tasted the wine,
smacking his lips, and then walked toward the bridegroom. I
looked down into the pitcher for the first time. It was filled with

fragrant wine. I turned to look at Jesus but He was speaking with His friends. I looked at His mother and she smiled and then quickly turned away.

Our Father, Hail Mary, Glory Be, Etc.
Additional clause: ...of thy womb, Jesus,
who changed water into wine.

Proclamation of the Kingdom - a Leper

And it came to pass when Jesus had fully ended these words, the people were in admiration at his doctrine. For he was teaching them as one having power, and not as the scribes and Pharisees. And when he was come down from the mountain, great multitudes followed him: And behold a leper came and adored him, saying: Lord, if thou wilt, thou canst make me clean. And Jesus stretching forth his hand, touched him, saying: I will, be thou made clean. And forthwith his leprosy was cleansed.

- Matthew 7:28 – 8:3

I had heard of Jesus but had not had the opportunity to hear Him speak. From a distance I could see the multitudes streaming toward the hillside where He was waiting. I was determined to move closer but fear held me at a distance from the people. I gathered as many articles of clothing as I could find and covered myself completely and moved slowly among the crowd.

His voice carried above the crowd. My heart burned within me as He spoke blessings that seemed to be for me alone. I was poor, hungry, sick, and people reviled me but His words wiped all my pain and bitterness away. I too like the birds of the air had always been provided for somehow all these years. He helped me to see all my blessings.

When He finished speaking many people went home while others tried to speak with Him. I stayed in my spot with my head down so I would not be noticed. A short time later two sandals appeared on the ground before me and I knew in my heart it was Him! I fell on my face saying, "Lord, if you will it, you can make me clean". He simply replied, "I do will it, be made clean". My face was still buried in the grass with tears rolling down my face as He walked away.

Our Father, Hail Mary, Glory Be, Etc.

Additional clause: ...of thy womb, Jesus,
who proclaimed the Kingdom of God.

The Transfiguration – St. James

And it came to pass, that as they were departing from him, Peter saith to Jesus:
Master, it is good for us to be here; and let us make three tabernacles, one for thee, and one for Moses, and one for Elias; not knowing what he said.

And when his disciples James and John had seen this, they said: Lord, wilt thou that we command fire to come down from heaven, and consume them? And turning, he rebuked them, saying: You know not of what spirit you are.

- Luke 9:33, 54-55

John and I were very upset with the Samaritans. They had refused to have Jesus come to their town on His way to Jerusalem. This meant that we would need to take to longer route to Jerusalem. Being upset, we asked Jesus if He would like us to teach the Samaritans a lesson by calling down fire from heaven to consume them. I realized before Jesus began to rebuke us, that we had crossed the line.

We knew instantly what Peter must have felt like when we were on the mountain just days before. Both John and I were frozen with fear when we saw Jesus glowing. We thought we were dreaming and couldn't believe we were watching Him speak with Moses and Elijah. However, when the cloud covered us and we heard the voice we were very much afraid. Then all of a sudden we saw Jesus alone.

It is amazing to think that after witnessing the Transfiguration of Jesus on the mountain we could utter something so stupid about the Samaritans. It goes to show how weak we really are and if we forget Jesus is truly God we can begin desiring to use His power for earthly things.

Our Father, Hail Mary, Glory Be, Etc.
Additional clause: ...of thy womb, Jesus,
who was transfigured on the mountain.

Institution of the Eucharist - Judas

Simon Peter therefore beckoned to him, and said to him:
Who is it of whom he speaketh? He therefore, leaning on the
breast of Jesus, saith to him: Lord, who is it? Jesus answered: He
it is to whom I shall reach bread dipped. And when he had dipped
the bread, he gave it to Judas Iscariot, the son of Simon. And after
the morsel, Satan entered into him. And Jesus said to him: That
which thou dost, do quickly. Now no man at the table knew to
what purpose he said this unto him. For some thought, because
Judas had the purse, that Jesus had said to him: Buy those things
which we have need of for the festival day: or that he should give
something to the poor. He therefore having received the morsel,
went out immediately. And it was night.

-John 13:24-30

They were all questioning Him, "is it I Lord". I was afraid of
giving myself away so I asked Him, "is it I master". I could no
longer call Him "Lord" after the episode in Capernaum with His
discourse about being the "bread come down from Heaven". I
stayed on with Him hoping that He would be the one to lead us to
victory over the empire. His words were always beautiful but they
were not what I wanted to hear. I decided it would be better if He
were out of the way.

His show in the Temple was bad. Everyone knew He was right but
no one wanted to hear it. It was easier to let things continue and
focus on overthrowing Rome. He didn't seem to mind when that
woman wasted all that oil that could have been used to buy
weapons but I still kept hope until this "Passover".

When He washed everyone's feet I knew that He was not the one
we were waiting on. Then, to make matters worse, He took bread,
blessed it, and broke it and gave it to all of us saying, "take, eat,
this is my body", and then likewise with the cup of wine. I took
the bread and immediately left the upper room. As I walked
toward the Temple to retrieve the guards I echoed the words of the

teachers that day in Capernaum, "How can this man give us His flesh to eat?"

Our Father, Hail Mary, Glory Be, Etc.
Additional clause: ...of thy womb, Jesus,
who was transfigured on the mountain.

The Sorrowful Mysteries through the eyes of St. John

The Agony in the Garden

And when he had dipped the bread, he gave it to Judas Iscariot, the son of Simon. And after the morsel, Satan entered into him. And Jesus said to him: That which thou dost, do quickly. He therefore having received the morsel, went out immediately. And it was night.

- John 13:26b-27, 30

After we finished with the dinner and sang the traditional songs the four of us walked out to Mount Olivet for evening prayers. Once we entered the Garden on Olivet Jesus told us to stay together and pray while He went on further. I was slightly frightened being out there on the hill so I placed myself between James and Peter with my back against the tree. I think we had too much wine because the conversation quickly died off and we all fell asleep.

When I awoke I was terrified. Jesus was standing above us, His eyes were afire while He was speaking to Peter and rebuking us all for sleeping. Some torches approached from behind us and I saw that Jesus was soaked from head to toe with sweat. He looked like a man who had just returned from battle.

Our Father, Hail Mary, Glory Be, Etc.
Additional clause: ...of thy womb, Jesus,
who sweat blood in agony.

The Scourging at the Pillar

Then therefore, Pilate took Jesus, and scourged him.
And I have been scourged all the day; and my chastisement
hath been in the mornings.

- John 19:1, Psalm 72:14

I secretly followed the group that took Jesus to Caiphas, the high priest. I stood quietly outside minding my own business and listening attentively. I thought I saw Peter there but he hid his face and ran off when Jesus looked at him. I followed them to the palace of Pontius Pilate. I could hear Pilate speaking. He was loud as men can be when they are scared. He asked Jesus some questions but I could not hear Our Lord's reply. Then I heard some laughter coming down the steps that emptied into the courtyard where I was standing. I stepped back in the shadows and caught my cloak on a thorn bush. Six men came out into the courtyard and surrounded Jesus. One of the soldiers began to remove Jesus' clothing while another bent down and picked up a whip. I shivered at the sight of the black leather whip. I had been told of how each strip of leather was weighed down by nails. The nails were meant to tear open the flesh of the person being scourged. They took Jesus who was now naked and placed his bound hands on a peg nailed to the pillar just out of normal reach. His feet barely touched the ground. I began to weep and had to cover my mouth to keep from being found when the first streaks of blood ran down Jesus' back. I could barely hear the whip. I watched helplessly as more streaks of dark red blood appeared on his back with each lash of the whip. I hid my eyes in my cloak.

Our Father, Hail Mary, Glory Be, Etc.
Additional clause: ...of thy womb, Jesus,
who was scourged for our offenses.

The Crowning of Thorns

And the soldiers platting a crown of thorns, put it upon his head; and they put on him a purple garment. And they came to him, and said: Hail, king of the Jews; and they gave him blows.

And they brought out the king's son, and put the crown upon him, and the testimony, and gave him the law to hold in his hand, and they made him king:

I will thresh your flesh with the thorns and briers of the desert.

- John 19:2-3, 2 Chronicles 23:11, Judges 8:7b

Silence filled the courtyard and I looked up. The soldiers had placed an old purple cloak on Jesus and were spitting at him and smacking him. He did not make a sound. They continued to taunt him. One soldier blindfolded him with a piece of cloth and the rest told Jesus to prophesy and tell them who had hit him. I stood motionless in the shadows. I was frozen with fear and my cloak was caught by the thorn bush. One of the soldiers noticed me standing by the bush and began to walk in my direction. I wanted to stay but I was too afraid. I began to run but my cloak was caught. It eventually ripped and I made my escape. The soldier yelled in my direction but he didn't chase me. I ran crying to Jesus' mother's house.

Our Father, Hail Mary, Glory Be, Etc.
Additional clause: ...of thy womb, Jesus,
who was crowned with thorns.

The Carrying of the Cross

And bearing his own cross, he went forth to that place which is called Calvary, but in Hebrew Golgotha.

All we like sheep have gone astray, every one hath turned aside into his own way: and the Lord hath laid on him the iniquity of us all.

- John19:17, Isaiah 53:6

After I woke Mary we went to find the other Mary who had washed Jesus' feet with her hair. The three of us walked toward Jerusalem. It was difficult to get through the crowds that were there for the Passover. We asked if anyone knew where Jesus of Nazareth might be. Some said that He had been freed but we found that it was another Jesus. A short while later a rumor spread through the crowd that the Romans were executing some men outside of the city and Jesus was one of them. We immediately headed towards Golgatha. On the way there we met the crowd. There was a whole Roman cohort following a man carrying a cross. I watched the cross He was carrying drop to the ground as He fell. I knelt down and saw, through the legs of the soldiers, that it was Jesus. We pushed Mary through the crowd shouting that the prisoners' mother would like to see Her son. The guards halted the procession for a moment and gave Mary a chance to talk to Jesus. I don't know what was said between them. When she returned to us she simply said, "Let us follow him to the end."

Our Father, Hail Mary, Glory Be, Etc.
Additional clause: ...of thy womb, Jesus,
who was made to carry the cross.

The Crucifixion and Death of Jesus

Now there stood by the cross of Jesus, his mother, and his mother's sister, Mary of Cleophas, and Mary Magdalen. When Jesus therefore had seen his mother and the disciple standing whom he loved, he saith to his mother: Woman, behold thy son. After that, he saith to the disciple: Behold thy mother. And from that hour, the disciple took her to his own. Afterwards, Jesus knowing that all things were now accomplished, that the scripture might be fulfilled, said: I thirst. Now there was a vessel set there full of vinegar. And they, putting a sponge full of vinegar and hyssop, put it to his mouth. Jesus therefore, when he had taken the vinegar, said: It is consummated. And bowing his head, he gave up the ghost.

John 19:25-30

When we arrived at the execution place the guards pushed the people back from the area. I felt sick to my stomach when I heard the steel hammer strike the nail. It is a sound I will never forget. Mary wrapped her arm around me and I buried my face in her mantle. When I finally looked up I saw Jesus had been placed between two criminals. The guards had moved on to the other side of the hill and were playing some sort of game so we moved closer to Jesus. Jesus and the man on His right were having a conversation. We couldn't hear so we moved closer. Some men were taunting Jesus from the ground and even the other crucified man shouted nasty things at Him. He hung there for a long time before He lifted His head and made eye contact with Mary and me. Tears streamed down my face as I looked at the man I loved so much. He had a crown of thorns embedded into His hair and bloody nails in His hands and feet. On one of the thorns hung a small piece of cloth, I looked at my cloak and realized it belonged to me. He smiled and began to pray.

Our Father, Hail Mary, Glory Be, Etc.
Additional clause: ...of thy womb, Jesus,
who died on the cross for us.

179

The Glorious Mysteries through the eyes of the Blessed Virgin Mary

The Resurrection

Mary Magdalen cometh, and telleth the disciples: I have seen the Lord, and these things he said to me. Now when it was late that same day, the first of the week, and the doors were shut, where the disciples were gathered together, for fear of the Jews, Jesus came and stood in the midst, and said to them: Peace be to you. And when he had said this, he shewed them his hands and his side. The disciples therefore were glad, when they saw the Lord. He said therefore to them again: Peace be to you. As the Father hath sent me, I also send you. When he had said this, he breathed on them; and he said to them: Receive ye the Holy Ghost.

Thou indeed, O most wicked man, destroyest us out of this present life: but the King of the world will raise us up, who die for his laws, in the resurrection of eternal life.

-John 20:18-22, 2 Maccabees 7:9

I knew in my heart that God had something special planned for his people. I knew that I would see my Son again one day but this surpassed all of my expectations. When Mary Magdalene arrived at my door out of breath and with an otherworldly glow about her, I knew something had happened. When she told me that she had spoken to Jesus, that He was alive, I fell to my knees and praised God. It was as if a thousand tiny daggers were removed from my heart in an instant.

That very evening Jesus visited me. We said nothing. We simply embraced and sat together for a while watching the sun set. He said that He had others to visit and that He must go. He gave me a kiss on the cheek like He always did since the time when He was a little boy and then vanished into the cool night air. I sat there recalling the events of the past thirty-three years. A shooting star streaked across the sky. I thought of the Magi.

Our Father, Hail Mary, Glory Be, Etc.
Additional clause: ...of thy womb, Jesus,
who rose from the dead.

The Ascension

And I send the promise of my Father upon you: but stay you in the city till you be endued with power from on high. And he led them out as far as Bethania: and lifting up his hands, he blessed them. And it came to pass, whilst he blessed them, he departed from them, and was carried up to heaven. And they adoring went back into Jerusalem with great joy.

God is ascended with jubilee, and the Lord with the sound of trumpet. Sing praises to our God, sing ye: sing praises to our king, sing ye. For God is the king of all the earth: sing ye wisely.

- Luke 24:49-52, Psalm 46 6-8

I saw Jesus more often after His resurrection than I had before. Many people visited me hoping to find Him at home. John had been staying with me lately, helping with chores mostly. He was always trying to persuade me to go listen to Jesus but I didn't want to bother Him. On the day *it* happened, through the grace of God, John had finally worn me down. I realized later that John wanted me to go because Jesus was speaking on Mount Olivet, the same place John had seen Him suffering before His crucifixion.

When we arrived there was an uneasy feeling about the crowd. They were pressing Jesus and asking if now was the time when He would restore Jerusalem to Israel. Those poor men were still thinking as men think and not as God thinks. He told them plainly that it was not for them to know the plans of the Father but to trust God in all things. He informed them once again that He must leave them so that He could send the Advocate. With that He stretched out His hands and blessed us. When we lifted our heads we saw Him rise slowly above the crowd. The entire crowd watched with their heads tilted back in a most uncomfortable position. Then all at once they were released from their trance like state. John heard some people mentioning my name so we quietly left the crowd and proceeded to John's home.

Our Father, Hail Mary, Glory Be, Etc.

Additional clause: ...of thy womb, Jesus,
who ascended into Heaven.

The Descent of the Holy Spirit

And when the days of the Pentecost were accomplished,
they were all together in one place: And suddenly there came a
sound from heaven, as of a mighty wind coming, and it filled the
whole house where they were sitting. And there appeared to them
parted tongues as it were of fire, and it sat upon every one of them:
And they were all filled with the Holy Ghost, and they began to
speak with divers tongues, according as the Holy Ghost gave them
to speak.

- Acts of the Apostles 2:1-4

We had been gathering in an upper room in Jerusalem. It was the
same room in which Jesus had established the Father's new
covenant and washed His disciples feet. When the feast of
Pentecost was at hand we were gathered there praying as we often
did. A strange howling sound could be heard but no one knew
where it was coming from. It became louder and louder as we
continued to pray. I was sitting on a chair in the midst of the
disciples of Jesus with John at my feet. The sound was deafening
like the sand storms of the desert yet the air in the room was
perfectly still. In an instant a large glowing mass was hovering
over our heads. It appeared to pulse and intensify with our prayers.
As we continued praying it began to change colors. It changed
from a cool, bluish-tint to a fiery red. It then divided itself and the
individual pieces came to rest above each of us. The sound of the
wind continued and we continued praying. Then with a flash, each
individual ball of fire dropped onto the person it was hovering
above. No one was hurt, everyone was at peace, and there was
perfect silence.

Our Father, Hail Mary, Glory Be, Etc.
Additional clause: ...of thy womb, Jesus,
who sent forth the Holy Spirit.

The Assumption of Mary

And there were given to the woman two wings of a great eagle, that she might fly into the desert unto her place

Thou that liftest me up from the gates of death, that I may declare all thy praises in the gates of the daughter of Sion. I will rejoice in thy salvation

- Revelation 12:14, Psalm 9:15-16a

Many of the apostles had gathered at John's home when they heard that I was nearing the end. They all gathered around me like they had on that morning of Pentecost. Mary Magdalene had been taking care of me for quite some time. I told them all that I loved them as if they were my own children and asked them to pray for me since my time was at hand. Everyone came close to the bed and began to pray over me. Again I heard the sound of rushing wind but no one else seemed to hear it. They continued to pray. Then, as if in a dream, Jesus appeared in the doorway. He smiled at me and walked over to the side of the bed and took my hand. He knelt down and kissed my hand and then my cheek as He had so many times before. He stood again and simply said, "follow me." When I began to get up all the people gathered there took a step back in amazement. Mary had tears in her eyes. Peter hugged John like a son and they all followed me out to the hillside. I gave them all a motherly embrace and with that I felt myself lifted up. I watched the men and women below me looking up as children do when admiring their mothers. My heart was moved with pity for them. I promised myself to spend eternity praying for all my adopted children.

Our Father, Hail Mary, Glory Be, Etc.
Additional clause: ...of thy womb, Jesus,
who assumed His Mother into Heaven.

The Crowning of Mary

And the temple of God was opened in heaven: and the ark of his testament was seen in his temple, and there were lightnings, and voices, and an earthquake, and great hail. And a great sign appeared in heaven: A woman clothed with the sun, and the moon under her feet, and on her head a crown of twelve stars:

The daughters of kings have delighted thee in thy glory. The queen stood on thy right hand, in gilded clothing; surrounded with variety.

- Revelation 11:19 - 12:1, Psalm 44:10

Many paintings have been created to capture this moment of beauty but earthly words cannot describe that which is heavenly. My crown is made up of my adopted children with the prize jewel being my Son. They, and He, are what make me Queen of Heaven and Earth. All glory goes to God for what He has done for me. I will always sit obediently at the right hand of my Son and intercede for any of His brothers or sisters who ask me to do so. By the grace of God I was permitted to bring Grace into the world. Now as the Heavenly Queen I lovingly distribute all the graces that come from my Son.

Our Father, Hail Mary, Glory Be, Etc.
Additional clause: ...of thy womb, Jesus,
who crowned His Mother as Queen.

Suggested Reading

Rosarium Virginis Maraie – John Paul II – Pauline Books & Media

Hail Holy Queen – Scott Hahn – Doubleday

The Way – St. Josemaria Escriva - Scepter
Furrow
The Forge

The World's First Love – Archbishop Fulton J. Sheen – Ignatius

Fr. Peyton's Rosary Book – Fr. Patrick Peyton – Ignatius

The Rosary: Chain of Hope – Fr. Benedict Groeschel, C.F.R. - Ignatius

The Catholic Answer Book of Mary – Fr. Peter Stravinskas – Our Sunday Visitor

A Protestant Pastor Looks at Mary – Charles Dickson – Our Sunday Visitor

Seven Day Bible Rosary – John F. Kippley – Couple to Couple League

The Imitation of Mary – Catholic Book Publishing Company

Total Consecration – St. Louis Marie de Montfort – Montfort Publications

33 Days to Morning Glory – Fr. Michael E Gaitley -

[1] Luke 1:38
[2] James 2:26
[3] Genesis 2:15
[4] 1 Thessalonians 5:17
[5] 1 Corinthians 13:7
[6] Matthew 3:3
[7] John 2:5
[8] Rosarium Virginis Mariae, Pope John Paul II
[9] Gaudium et spes 22
[10] Mark 14:38
[11] Luke 23:34
[12] Luke 22:19
[13] Philippians 2:8
[14] 1 Peter 4:8 (RSV)
[15] Cf. Philippians 2:12
[16] John 15:5
[17] Cf. Philippians 4:13
[18] 1 Corinthians 2:9
[19] Cf. Matthew 18:3
[20] Galatians 2:20 (RSV)
[21] Luke 2:35
[22] John 2:5 (RSV)
[23] Mark 1:15
[24] Mark 14:36
[25] Proverbs 13:24
[26] Proverbs 3:12
[27] Matthew 10:37
[28] Matthew 28:20
[29] Luke 1:52
[30] Revelation 12:17
[31] Baltimore Catechism
[32] Luke 1:38
[33] *Brave heart - Mel Gibson*
[34] 1 Corinthians 15:55
[35] Luke 2:11
[36] Luke 2:29

[37] John 3:30

[38] Romans 6:4

[39] Mark 10:9

[40] John 6:54

[41] Romans 8:28

[42] Luke 23:14-16

[43] Psalm 21:17

[44] Luke 9:23

[45] John 19:25-26

[46] Psalm 30:6

[47] John 11:25

[48] Revelation 21:5

[49] Mark 9:28

[50] Luke 2:52

[51] James 1:15

[52] Genesis 3:22

[53] Saint Gregory of Nazianzus, Bishop

[54] Psalm 103:15, RSV 104:15

[55] *Screwtape Letters, C.S. Lewis*

[56] Genesis 3:6

[57] Hebrews 12:4

[58] Luke 22:48

[59] Isaiah 53:7

[60] Isaiah 50:7

[61] Isaiah 53:6

[62] John 19:30 RSV

[63] Revelation 7:14

[64] Psalm 16:8

[65] Matthew 6:24

[66] Revelation 12:17

[67] Sirach 24:41-42

[68] 1 Peter 3:1,7

[69] Mark 5:36

[70] Matthew 4:17

[71] Matthew 26:41

[72] Ephesians 6:12

[73] Hosea 13:14

[74] 1 Corinthians 6:19

[75] 1 Corinthians 7:4

[76] 1 Corinthians 7:14

[77] Matthew 18:20

[78] Acts of the Apostles 1:8

[79] John 6:61

[80] 2 Corinthians 5:7

[81] Tantum Ergo - St. Thomas Aquinas

[82] John 20:29

[83] Cf. Leviticus 12:6

[84] Cf. Luke 2:51-52

[85] Anima Christi

[86] Matthew 4:17

[87] Cf. St. Augustine CCC 129 fnt. 107

[88] *Lumen Gentium* 11, CCC 1324)

[89] Malachi 1:11

[90] Colossians 1:23-24

[91] Isaiah 53:5

[92] Acts of the Apostles 26:15

[93] Galatians 2:20 RSV

[94] Psalm 84:11

37512955R00113

Made in the USA
Lexington, KY
04 December 2014